The Easy Way to Write a Novel That Sells

ROB PARNELL

To Robyn.

CONTENTS

PART THREE – The 30 Day Formula

BONUS:
A Proven Strategy for Getting Your Novel Taken Seriously by Agents and Publishers

AUTHOR'S NOTE

This book is written in three distinct parts – for a very good reason. It is imperative that you read them in the right order.

You may be tempted to skip ahead to the techniques outlined in Part Three, especially if you're a professional. You're probably eager to get on and write your novel in less than a month. That's understandable.

But there's a catch.

You see, if you don't first read Part One and Part Two – then Part Three won't work for you. At least it won't work as well as it should – even if you've written novels before.

Writing a novel can be easy, but there's something important you must learn first. In order to write quickly and well you need to be in the right state of mind.

This may sound glib and obvious but it is not.

Part One is about reprogramming your thinking. If you read all that is said, carefully and mindfully, you will know the best way to think, the best mindset to acquire, before you start – before you put one word on paper.

Part Two is about learning the art of commercial fiction writing. Many would be professionals never learn that there is a correct way to construct fiction for publication. Writing sellable fiction is an art. Anybody can write fiction, but only a few can write commercial fiction – which is very different. You need to know the difference!

Therefore, my sincere advice is: do not skip ahead!

By reading Parts One and Two first, Part Three will be all the more powerful and helpful to you, especially when you reach the midway point of your novel. If you've tried writing novels before, you'll know when I mean: the point at which most writers stop or give up.

If you're serious about being a writer, you can't afford to do that. So, for the moment, keep reading in a linear fashion.

Oh, and don't start writing yet either – not until you've reached the end of the book!

Don't worry, there's plenty of time. Chances are, you may have spent several months thinking about writing your novel anyway. What difference will a few days make?

Sit back; take it easy and read on.

PART ONE

The Write Way to Think

INTRODUCTION

Don't Skip the Prologue!

There are certain folks out there who never read the introduction to a book.

I've never understood why.

Usually the introduction, like the prologue of a novel, or the first five minutes of a TV show, contains the most crucial information necessary to make sense of the rest of the program.

So it is in this case.

I believe you'll be asking some questions at this point. I'm going to answer a few of them now, before we get started.

What Can I Expect From This Book?

Simply put, I'm going to show you in simple, straightforward steps, the easiest and quickest way to write an outstanding piece of novel length fiction. Say between 80,000 and 120,000 words. All down on paper within 30 days or less.

Sounds like a daunting prospect, doesn't it? I bet you're thinking things like:

That's not possible, is it?
How will I have the time? □□
Will I have the dedication?
Surely I don't have the talent!

I want you to banish these doubts from your mind. Completely. Trust me.

Why Should I Trust You?

I have been writing novels, short stories, plays, screenplays and articles for most of my life. I've written almost fifty books and courses on writing that have been published all over the world. I speak at seminars and on radio shows about writing. For my sins I have been labeled the world's foremost writing guru - an accolade I still cringe over when I hear it!

But more importantly, I've been involved with writers and writers' groups for over thirty years, more especially with the subscribers to my website, *The Easy Way to Write*, for the last fifteen years, where I have taught commercial fiction writing to over a million students.

I've worked with amateur and professional writers of all types and temperaments on all sorts of writing projects - and this has given me highly valuable knowledge. It is largely this, as well as my own experience and that of other leading figures in the industry that I have drawn on to put together this groundbreaking book.

How Can Writing a Novel Be Easy?

Let me explain.

Since the beginning of the written word, there's been a tacit understanding between all of us that somehow writing is hard work.

We all have this picture of a lone writer, hunched over a desk, poring over pieces of paper, quill pen scratching away, brow furrowed and deep in contemplation.

This is an enduring image – but it is also a negative one.

Banish it from your mind.

Why?

Because, like a lot of the myths about writing, having the wrong mental images can actually hinder the writing process for you.

A large part of this book is about undoing common misconceptions – so that properly "reprogrammed", you can go on to write your own novel quickly and easily.

I believe this book is also a first. Not only does it mentally prepare you for the great task of writing a novel, it gives much of the new wisdom available regarding rules, tips and techniques of great fiction writing. So that, not only will you write your novel quickly and easily, if you follow these simple rules it will most likely be a good, competent and ultimately sellable novel.

So How Does it Work?

There is an easier way to write. It's got nothing to do with talent, skill or dedication.

It has to do with attitude.

Some of the things you will read soon may seem radical. You may disagree with certain points. However, bear in mind that if you do take on board at least some of the suggestions I make, I promise that you will find writing your first novel – or your next novel if it's not your first – one whole lot easier. Guaranteed.

Writers are a stubborn species. They would rather stick with their own way of doing things, even if it never gets them what they want. It can take years for a simple truth to dawn on a writer and for him or her to change their ways. I know, it's happened to me.

This book is for those who want to bypass all the common mistakes that other writers make and move in to the fast lane as soon as possible. This book is for writers who want to learn how to feel like a professional from day one – and perform accordingly. This book is especially for writers who want to write a first draft of their novel in thirty days or less.

But Some Professionals Take a Year or Two to Write a Novel, Don't They?

That's true, and this book is as much for them too.

Much of the wisdom in this book is new. In part, it is an extension of new-age psychology and our 21st Century understanding of how the mind works.

A Short History Lesson

Long ago, writing was uncommon. The forerunner of the system we now use in the West appeared spontaneously around five thousand years ago in the Mesopotamian basin, in what is now (perhaps ironically) Iraq.

Ancient scribes chiseled away at stones to record business transactions in Sumerian script – a series of dashes and grooves. Later a more pictographic form of the language took hold and was used to tell the legends of Gilgamesh and Enlil – heroic tales of gods, adventure and mystery - to create probably the first novel length fiction in the world!

The dislocated Jews of the Old Testament then began to record their oral traditions – stories that emphasized their relationship with their god, Yahweh – originally written as YHWH and meaning literally: "the name that cannot be spoken."

The Egyptians used complex hieroglyphics to honor their dead and glorify their kings.

You see, from the beginning writing has been associated with gods and mystery and at least some form of storytelling.

This is because, at its heart, writing is about trying to make sense of our relationship with the profound mysteries of life. As soon as we crawled out of the primordial swamp and gained consciousness, we had questions.

Why are we here?

Is there a God?

And if there is, what does he want from us?

These were the questions our ancestors tried to answer (and we're still trying to answer today). They recorded their insights and information so that they could pass them on to subsequent generations. In this sense, writing has always been an act of benevolence.

But for centuries, the skill of writing, and reading for that matter, was possessed by only the few. To the uneducated, the apparent exchange of information via simple marks and symbols must have seemed nothing short of magical.

During the Middle Ages, those that could afford it sent their children to monasteries where they were taught to read and write. Monks would spend their lives copying out religious texts, sometimes adding or deleting passages for reasons lost. In this way, books have been passed through the ages, one word at a time.

Yes, in former days, writing was laborious, perhaps even tedious. It probably wasn't much different when the Industrial Revolution happened and suddenly education became available to all.

Thankfully, things are different now.

Today, we all learn to read and write as a matter of course. Our modern minds have a different relationship with the written word. When we see a headline in the newspaper we don't process the fact that we're reading, we just see the headline and get the sense of it. We see the picture that the words represent.

That makes us lucky, privileged even. We understand the magic of words so completely that we take them for granted. We sometimes forget the awesome power of the written word. How it can inspire worship, spark wars, build nations, crush empires, and destroy hope. How it can offer us salvation or despair as easily as it can be used to give us entertainment, to make us laugh or cry.

Everything around us, all the technology that makes our lives richer, starts with writing. Whether it's a philosophical or scientific idea, or perhaps a business plan or a movie script – everything starts with writing.

In effect, everything man-made is caused by the act of taking words out of our heads and putting them onto paper. That's how we make things real.

Nowadays, our attitude towards the written word is different from our forebears. It is no longer seen as mysterious. It's seen as a tool for communication – unglamorous and functional. It's seen as a right too, something we all must have to make our way in the world.

New technologies like the Internet have enabled us to transfer information in a way that was impossible even a couple of decades ago. This has meant that a new understanding of many things – including something as mundane as writing – has been able to emerge and be proliferated.

As well as being a compilation of over three decades of personal experience, good and bad, this book is essentially a synthesis of the newest and most effective techniques known on the subject of fiction writing. I believe it is probably the first of many books that will continue to outline these techniques in detail.

Okay, What Now?

Talk to any successful novelist and they will invariably say the same thing. They wish they'd "got the hang" of writing novels sooner in their careers. Because, to be blunt, that's where the money is.

Also – from a creative point of view, it's where the greatest satisfaction lies. There is no better feeling than holding a finished book in your hands and thinking, I did this! This is increasingly true whether the book is in print or available as an ebook. These days there's far less stigma attached to self publishing, especially when Amazon authors are routinely outselling traditional authors in the modern book marketplace.

Now – it's your turn.

CHAPTER ONE

It's All in the Mind

If you are reasonably well educated, or even if not, everything you need to write an enduring novel-length piece of fiction is inside of you. You already possess the talent and the necessary skills. All you have to do it access them.

How can you do that?

Read on.

The brain is a complex machine. It takes in far more than most of us realize. Under hypnosis, people can relate the contents of an entire book in rich detail that, in a waking state, they'd forgotten they'd read. Psychologists say that, at some deep level, the mind actually remembers everything it experiences.

If you think about it, that's incredible.

It's well accepted nowadays that the brain is split into two levels: the conscious and the subconscious. We use the conscious while we're awake to do the things we have to do. Eat, work, communicate, play games, etc. The conscious mind is always active, trying to solve problems, experiencing the moment, helping us to cope with daily life. It's a miracle in action.

It has a flaw though.

The conscious mind can only focus on one or two things at a

time. More than that and it starts to complain. The most common way this manifests itself is via stress, worry and later, physical symptoms like tiredness and muscle pain can develop.

The subconscious is different. It is a vast storehouse of memory, experience and capabilities. It hardly impinges on our waking lives because the human brain simply could not stand the overload of information it carries. Most of all we know, feel or have experienced is kept shielded from us – until our conscious mind needs to access it.

Techniques like driving a car, playing an instrument or performing a routine task are housed in the subconscious. When we access those activities, the conscious mind is overridden so that we seem to be able to perform on "auto-pilot". Again, the subconscious takes over because the conscious mind could not process the information quickly enough for us to keep up.

Anyone who has learned to drive or play an instrument – and remembers how hard it was at first – will be familiar with this phenomenon.

Similarly, the subconscious can be taught how to write novels. Once the technique is embedded into the subconscious, it will stay there – ready for you to access at any time.

Once you have learned how this works – which the rest of the book will show you – you will be able to write well, quickly and easily. In fact, it may not seem like real writing at all - because it will be the subconscious that will be writing for you.

Accept this simple fact, and you're half way there.

The Journey Begins

There's another complication.

Because the conscious mind is not very good at dealing with things, it needs a failsafe.

Consequently, consciousness creates an objective observer of itself to comment and guide us through life. The word "objective" is in italics because, as I will prove to you, it's actually not very objective at all.

Each of us is subject to an endless internal monologue.

Let's call it *The Commentator*.

The Commentator is constantly telling us what we should and shouldn't do, what we're capable of and what we're not, and even what we should think.

This would be fine if The Commentator was wise and caring and always looking after our best interests. Sadly, it's not. It's usually a mess of conflicting opinions and prejudices that do nothing much to help us, but rather make us feel inadequate and inferior.

The Commentator is like one of these brainless DJs that doesn't like silence. It prattles on whether you want it to or not. It's forever analyzing incoming data, trying to make sense of the facts and events as it sees them. It tries constantly to put things into context for you, reinforcing what you already believe.

The problem is that The Commentator isn't always the good friend you might suppose.

It's cunning and smart, but doesn't like change. It's always on the look out for anything that might reinforce your worldview – however negative that might be.

If you believe something – however false – The Commentator will do anything its power to find evidence for the truth of it. The Commentator is clever enough to screen out any information to the contrary so effectively that you may not even see it.

For instance, if you believe you are not capable of writing a novel and that it should be left to Stephen King, James Patterson or Patricia Cornwell because they have talent and you don't, The Commentator is only too glad to agree with you. Of course it is. The Commentator's main function is to stop you from doing anything, to make things seem impossible, and to prove that most activities are not worthwhile. It will come up with all sorts of reasons why you have no talent, no time, or lack the motivation.

Quite why The Commentator does this for most of us is a mystery. I assume it's trying to get back to a state of blissful inertia where it can relax and do nothing – back to the womb perhaps. But of course, that's not what you want. You want to do things, achieve things – big things -and have fun doing them.

There is hope.

There are a lot of books around these days that can help you change the way The Commentator speaks to you. I recommend that you read some if you haven't already. I list a few at the back of this book.

In the mean time, I'll let you know the trick.

You have to consciously be aware of your Commentator and continuously redirect it into telling you positive things. Each time you catch yourself thinking a negative thought like, All people in management positions are incompetent, you have to check yourself. State the opposite position, or at least try to have a point of view that is more rational and considered like, There are good and bad managers, some of whom are intelligent and thoughtful and others that struggle in their positions.

The expert thinking is that, after about two weeks of this activity, you can completely reprogram your mind to believe exactly what you tell it. It's hard – and you'll be surprised just how negative your internal voice can be, but the effort is worth it.

Because, the sad truth is, if you don't really believe that you will write a novel, your Commentator isn't going to let you finish it.

Getting The Commentator straight is vitally important for your writing for another good reason.

It's the same voice that will write your novel.

Therefore, you need the voice to be healthy, mature and insightful. You don't want it bitter, prejudiced or loaded with inappropriate baggage.

That's why I recommend you spend at least two weeks – or at least the next couple of days - from now, this moment, clearing your head, nurturing your Commentator with good thoughts, before you start any work on your novel.

Good Writing

I've known enough writers to know that the best writing comes from a clear and balanced mind.

A good novel requires balance. Let me give you an example.

If, for instance, you feel strongly that there is no God and that fact is an integral part of your plot, you will write in plot twists and characterizations that reflect your view.

However, your reader may not agree with that view. Already you have a problem.

Because your plot does not have balance – that is, the opposing view that there is a God – your reader senses your presence whilst reading. This is one example of authorial intrusion.

Even though you don't specifically state your case, the reader feels your overbearing presence and probably feels lectured to.

The only mature way to make a point is to have opposing arguments in your story too.

For every passionate atheist in your story, for instance, you should have an equally strong Christian or Catholic. Then you have balance. The reader trusts your worldview. And creating and building on that trust is what being a good writer is all about.

Balance has to start within you. You need to clear the decks, so to speak. Try to be as centered as possible. This doesn't mean you have to wait until you're totally mentally healthy before you begin but – hey, maybe it's not such a bad idea.

From a balanced mind comes wisdom and from wisdom comes certainty – and a sense of certainty will help to banish self-doubt.

Of course, it won't banish it completely. There will always be a part of you that doubts you can succeed – at anything.

The trick is to go on regardless, sure of your abilities and intent. The rest will follow.

Preparing Yourself

Ironically, suppressing The Commentator is easy - if you never stretch yourself.

If at the end of a couple of weeks, you still have a hundred nagging doubts, try to see them as good, positive signs that you are about to embark on something exciting. That the fear you feel is actually anticipation in another form.

The fact is The Commentator is trying to protect you from harm, rejection and disappointment. It probably knows that you don't react well to these things!

But remember, that your particular Commentator is not only your responsibility but it is something you put inside your head – a long time ago, perhaps when you were a child. Perhaps your parents helped put it there. Worse, the people around you are still concurring with The Commentator on a daily basis, reinforcing its power over you.

The only way to quash The Commentator is to systematically take each doubting phrase it utters and consciously turn it around.

For instance, every time you hear yourself say, I can't do this, say to yourself at least five times, I CAN do this. I know I can, raising the intensity of your voice each time.

It's a very simple technique that some of us – the most successful – probably use without thinking. Naturally successful people are unconsciously aware that in order for us to be sure of our abilities, we need constant reinforcement and encouragement, especially if we're not receiving it from external forces!

I can vouch that though the technique is simple, it really does work. The subconscious likes repetition. If you say something to yourself enough times, the brain starts to believe it. I don't know why. It just does.

Practical Advice

Go for a walk - often. You'll find that the rhythmic nature of walking has a profound hypnotic effect on the brain. Repeat to yourself positive phrases in time with your steps.

Phrases like:

* *I can write a book easily. No problem.*
* *I'm excellent at plotting.*
* *My dialogue is totally convincing.*
* *I'm a great wordsmith.*
* *I can see the whole book in my mind.*

Say them over and over, like a mantra, until you're not even aware of the words.

You'll find that positive affirmations like this lodge in the subconscious mind. Soon, the subconscious comes to believe them, so that later, perhaps when it comes to dealing with a "hard" part in your novel, your mind thinks you already have the skills to overcome it.

Strange but true: if you think you can overcome a problem, you usually can.

Confidence

Try to use these techniques to banish any kind of self-doubt. I say this because it's probably the biggest handicap writers have to deal with. I've seen it happen a hundred, a thousand times. Critics, agents and publishers do not necessarily destroy a writer's career. But self-doubt will do it every time.

I admit that to those unfamiliar with the above techniques, and to the cynical, the idea that anything is achievable just because you decide it is might seem naive.

However, as I said in the introduction, I'm not asking for your belief. I'm after a momentary suspension of disbelief.

If you are familiar with fiction writing, you will know that is an accepted feature of the whole game of writing. It is the job of the fiction writer to get the reader to let go of their logical mind and go with the flow of the writer. It's a subtle form of hypnosis.

The point is, if the reader does not suspend their disbelief — especially in more fanciful tales — there is very little chance that the reader will enjoy the experience or get anything out of it.

Consequently, I ask that you also suspend your disbelief for the rest of this book. I hope you'll find that by doing so, even just temporarily, that taking on board some of the things I will say, the effect on you may be tremendous — especially the effect on your writing.

When I make some of the upcoming statements, it is not an opportunity for your logical mind to jump in, disagree and start thinking of counter arguments.

Here's a Secret

You can write a novel quickly if you truly believe you can.

The process of truly believing may take a little longer than you'd like (at least till the end of this book!) but the above statement is true of all writers. Those who never question their ability to write good novels, just do it.

Those other writers, who doubt their ability, don't.

It's obvious if you think about it. The only reason novelists are writing novels is that experience has taught them they know they can write them.

The one-novel writer is a bit of cliché.

Harper Lee is probably the most famous. She got a Pulitzer Prize for *To Kill a Mockingbird*, a masterful piece of semi-autobiographical fiction. What happened? She never wrote another book. Why?

Did she lack the talent? Certainly not.

My guess would be she simply didn't believe she could do any better. Perhaps she never tried, never believing she could do it.

Soon I'll be dealing with lots more of these sorts of issues. Like the definition of talent, and whether you have it. And other pertinent issues like finding the time to write, dealing with distractions and the fear of ridicule.

But for now, I want to talk about some essential, important tools you will need to write a great novel quickly. I'm not talking about expensive tools either, like computers or special software.

No, these are free, and you already own them.

Relaxation

Being a relaxed person is one of the key elements of being a good writer.

Sure, you can write when you're angry, resentful, bitter, even joyous, exhilarated and euphoric. You can write when you're drunk or stoned too, but that doesn't mean what you produce is any good.

Usually writing produced in anything less than a relaxed state comes across as naive, overdone or immature. Or just plain bad.

This is because your emotions taint the words, the sentences and the paragraphs you are writing. The reader can tell that you were feeling a certain way when you were writing, because the reader can sense the distorted logic that these emotions bring to a work.

Readers want objectivity from their writers. They also want excitement, thrills and emotion but they won't accept these things from a writer they think is being self-indulgent. Writing that is not coming from a balanced, objective, relaxed mind will almost always seem self-indulgent.

That's true of any writing, fiction or otherwise.

So, you owe it to yourself to get your head together, as they say.

And the easiest way I know of doing that is to meditate.

Meditation

For some reason, in polite company nowadays, meditation is a bit of a dirty word.

Perhaps there's a residual stigma attached to it leftover from the 70s when the only people who meditated were the Beatles and dropped-out hippies who wanted to get in touch with their "higher" selves. New age practitioners of meditation have to deal with this stigma when selling the idea to people unimpressed by the association with long-haired gurus sitting cross-legged on a mountain top.

Tell friends that you meditate and they'll often laugh, or at least look at you oddly. Tell strangers and they give you a fixed smile – and start to back away. Tell your parents and they fear the worst.

I don't know why this is.

It's a great thing to do. It costs nothing and it makes you feel better than anything else in the world. Better than coffee, better than sex, better than a walk along the beach. Because it's all these things - and more.

Try This Once. Twice If You Like It

The following is an amalgam of various techniques I've studied. It's basically a cross between what Zen monks are said to do and a bit of the de Silva technique, with a smidge of self-hypnosis thrown in. I find it works for me.

Try it yourself. Only takes ten minutes.

Sit down, or lie down, get comfortable, whatever, don't get too hung up on it. I know a lot of people aren't comfortable with meditation because they feel silly and self-conscious. If you're like that, just relax and tell yourself you're going to do yourself some good.

Say to yourself,

A little meditation will make me feel a lot better.

Then repeat this phrase about five times. Mean it, or at least sound sincere enough to fool your subconscious, which is easily done.

Close your eyes.

Breathe softly and slowly three times, slower with each breath.

Begin a countdown from ten to one, breathing once for each number. Between the numbers, think certain phrases like:

When I reach zero I will be more relaxed than ever before.

Ten: Relax totally

Nine: My whole body is going numb

Eight: Every care and problem is dissolving

Seven: I feel centered and calm

Six…

– well, you get the idea. Make up your own phrases – they'll be a lot more powerful than the ones I suggest.

At zero, imagine that you're floating, unconscious of your body. This is hard I know.

It's usually about now you get an itch or you become aware of what you must look like.

Don't worry. Scratch that itch and carry on. It's no big deal.

You may need a few sessions before you feel anything like relaxed. Keep at it. The rewards are enormous.

While you're floating – on water, in space, on a cloud, whatever - try to push away all of your thoughts. Muffle them, imagine them drifting away like clouds. If they won't go – gently enclose them in an imaginary blanket and softly push them away.

Then – and this is the hard part – tell yourself to think of nothing.

Say, the word Silence to yourself, a few times. My experience is that, if it comes at all, the silence only last for a few seconds if you're lucky. At some stage, The Commentator will always step in and say something inane. Push it away.

I've found that it's these moments of silence that really benefit the mind – no matter how short or fleeting they are. It's said by gurus that within these moments of silence, there is a deep well of joy.

It's apparently what Zen Masters are trying to reach. A state of Nirvana.

Those guys spend their whole lives trying to achieve it. Don't beat yourself up if nothing happens for you immediately. The effort of relaxing totally, even for very short periods, can bring enormous benefit in the short and long term.

After a few minutes, count yourself back out, from one to ten. As you do, tell yourself you'll feel much better, more alive, but more relaxed than ever before when you open your eyes.

Ten minutes a day is usually enough. Fanatics suggest longer and more often but that's not always practical for most of us.

It's a particularly useful tool if you have a lot of creative work to do and either don't feel up to it or you are so stressed about it you can't start. In the middle of the meditative session, tell yourself you have all the time in the world to finish things. This will help you to cope.

Any form of conscious meditation will make you feel better and help you to start work feeling more confident and self-possessed. I recommend you start any creative session this way.

Visualization

I shall be returning to this topic later on, in a different context. For the moment I want to talk about it for the purposes of relaxation.

Creative visualization is a well documented, well researched technique that follows on from meditation. It can help the mind and body in all kinds of areas, not least relaxation.

It's a bit like dreaming while you're awake – or at least trying to. The idea is to create images in your mind that benefit you emotionally and physically. Imaginary landscapes are a favorite, as these can relax your mind and bring peace.

If you want to try it, do a similar countdown as with the above meditation sequence and then imagine that you're somewhere else – on a beach for example.

Choose a particular place you have pleasant and relaxing memories of. Pretend that you're there. Imagine the whole thing, using all the senses. Try to visualize actual objects like pebbles and wooden benches. See the colors, feel the elements around you, like breezes and the touch of water. Try to experience all the sensations associated with being in another space and time.

Again, this is hard for a beginner. But with practice this is not only a beneficial activity, it can help you in other ways, as it teaches you to notice details - definitely something that will help you in your writing.

Conclusion

All this may seem a million miles away from writing your novel. It's not. As with most important things, preparation is essential to a profitable outcome.

A little time spent on the above activities will help you focus on the important information coming up, and ultimately, make writing your novel much easier.

Now for a well kept secret...

CHAPTER TWO

The Secret to Being Creative

In the third section of this book, I'm going to be guiding you through a thirty day period that you may want to use to write your novel.

For now, we need to take what we've learned in the first chapter and take it to the next logical step. This book is about progress. Each chapter is part of a journey you must make with your mind to achieve the ultimate aim – to be the kind of person who can write a novel in thirty days or less.

The next step in the process is to take a break.

Yep, you read it right. Do nothing, relax, and take it easy. For a few days at least.

I know you probably bought this book because you wanted to get started straightaway.

Don't. You're not ready. Believe me, writing the novel is going to be a hell of a lot easier if you do it my way. Besides, you can spend the time reading the rest of this book!

Whatever you do – don't start writing your novel! That would be a disaster.

I know from personal experience and watching a whole lot of writers that the worst thing to do is to launch yourself into writing a novel without being properly prepared.

You see, the real reason why novels are said to take so long to write is that each time you take a break from writing, you have to mentally shift back into "writing mode".

This can take anything from ten minutes to several weeks each time you do it.

The trick is to be in this "writing mode" continually for as long as you're writing your novel. This doesn't mean you have to write continually 24/7 for thirty days. Far from it. Two or three hours a day should be enough to achieve the task – but only if you're mentally prepared.

This mental preparation is a skill that must be learned.

And it can be learned best if you are mentally healthy.

I intimated at the end of the last chapter, mentally healthy means mentally relaxed and clear. And one of the best ways to achieve mental health more quickly is to make a conscious effort to be more physically healthy.

This doesn't mean being in peak condition – although that might help. It means being comfortable with your body so that it doesn't act as a distraction. If it does, you'll find you won't be able to concentrate for the time that you spend writing.

So, for the next few days, try not to think about your novel for a while. In fact, do the opposite. Push the idea of it away. Whenever you catch yourself dwelling on certain aspects of it – or any kind of writing for that matter - banish those thoughts from your mind.

Don't worry; it will all come back when you want it to. And it will be better, stronger and more urgent.

You need to begin to trust your subconscious. Believe that it remembers everything and that, if you don't force it, everything you need to remember will come back to you at the right time, exactly when you need it.

On Notebooks – an Aside

Most writers, early on in their career, are advised that a good writer always carries around a notebook to write down ideas and stray thoughts.

At this point, novices will rush out and purchase an A6 pad, or anything small enough to put in the pocket, and begin scribbling at various points during the day for, oh, a couple of weeks at most, before the novelty wears off.

I once did a straw poll to see how many writers I knew had notebooks. Less than one in ten. Then I asked if those with notebooks actually used the ideas they wrote down.

About a quarter said they did.

I think the message is that, yes, ideas are fleeting – but if they are, perhaps they're also not worth recording!

I think notebooks are good from one angle. They help the novice translate the world around them into written words. Beyond that, most professional writers make all their notes during their writing time – and may have tons of them – but they are almost always relevant, rather than vague scribbling made in the middle of the night or on the spur of the moment.

Sometimes you may feel you have an idea so overwhelming that you have to write it down. That's different. Go for it.

But generally, I've found that good ideas have a habit of resurfacing. Very good ones just won't go away!

You may feel different. Keep a notebook if it's important to you. I do. I have dozens of them full of ideas that I never use. Sometimes I look back at these so-called pearls of wisdom and think: well, if I get desperate I'll use something here. Though it hasn't happened yet!

I Said Let Go!

If you're finding it hard to let go of your writing, try this:

Put everything you've ever written in to a cardboard box. If you've been prolific you might need many boxes or a trunk. If you're a professional, you might need a room.

The principle is the same. Take everything – all the manuscripts, the folders, the files, the odd bits of paper, even the envelopes and scraps – and, here's the important bit, tape down the box, seal the trunk, lock the door - firmly. Hide the box or trunk somewhere inaccessible. Under stairs, in the back bedroom, or in the shed. If you're lucky enough to have a writing room, lock it and give the key to someone else.

Get it out of your life.

Forget about it. Release yourself from your writing. Let it go, completely.

This may sound radical - but it sends a clear message to your subconscious that this time – it's over. You and writing have had it. You never want to think about it again.

How do you feel?

Panicked? Relieved? Free?

Whatever you're feeling, enjoy it. It'll probably be a new sensation, and a welcome one.

Now, it's time to…

Get Your Self Together

There are many ways to do this, many of which require time, or at least some effort.

My advice would be to take the path of least resistance. For just a few days, simply try to be nice to yourself.

Eat well – less meat, lots of vegetables, drink juice, get loads of sleep.

Go walking, do some gardening. Visit the beach.

Cut down on the coffee. Go without the booze. I know it's hard to change. Impossible, and impractical sometimes. But if you can slow down the rhythm of your life for maybe even a short while, it'll be worth it.

If you find it hard to let go, don't knock yourself out. That's hardly the point of the exercise. Just try everyday at least once to relax and feel as though you have no cares and worries, and that nothing really matters.

At your day job, if you have one, try to take everything a little easier. Tell your workmates to stop stressing you out. Tell your boss you've discovered you're more productive if you take off every ten minutes of the hour to relax. Okay, this might not go down very well – but actually it is a proven fact. Try it on your manager. He/she might even agree with you.

If not, who cares?

In the great scheme of things, nothing really does matter, does it? Not when you work for other people anyway. None of us are indispensible, as much as we might want to believe that we are.

Life goes on – and will go on without you.

Think about that. Dwell on it.

Is your job really that important?

Honestly? Or do you just think it is?

If it wasn't for the money, would you even bother turning up?

You can take a break, can't you? Just a short one.

You don't really have to care so much and work hard all the time, do you?

Relax.

Take it easy.

Think happy thoughts. Read an uplifting book – a self-help book ideally, something that will help unclog your thinking.

Do something unusual. Go swimming. Find a new park, walk amongst flowers! Enjoy the moment, wonder at the beauty and miraculous nature of the universe…

But, whatever you do, don't think about writing!

Some Tips on Being Healthy

I'm no fitness freak, and I'm certainly no Adonis anymore - though my wife disagrees! But I've picked up a few things along the way that seem to add up to a better way of living. More conducive to creativity, anyway. As far as I'm concerned, that's the only criterion that matters.

I don't advocate total abstinence from anything bad. Far from it. People who know me would find that hypocritical! Oftentimes I've noticed that being happy keeps people healthier than any strict diet or athletic regimes. I'm waiting to see concrete evidence that supports this theory but I'm sure there's something to it!

Here are some techniques you might like to try:

Restrict yourself to drinking only water before noon, and only fruit juice thereafter.

This is something I picked up from *Fit for Life* written by Harvey and Marilyn Diamond. For some reason which I've forgotten (they do explain it in the book) it helps clear the mind and settle the digestion.

As does being a vegetarian.

Don't make that dismissive noise! Listen up.

The trouble with eating meat is that the body wasn't built to process it. There is much evidence to suggest that our bodies were designed to be vegetarian. The shape of our teeth, our digestive juices, the intestinal tract process vegetable matter perfectly. Not so with meat. Meat is hard for the body to deal with. Consequently, eating large amounts of it can make you tired and listless, sapping your energy completely. Not good when you need to concentrate on writing..

Restrict your intake of tea, coffee, fizzy drinks and alcohol.

Drink a lot of water and herbal teas.

Avoid salt - it makes you lethargic and over thirsty.

Get away from it all. There's nothing quite like a long walk in the countryside. If there's no countryside near you, visit parks or the beach. If you're in the middle of a city where nothing like this exists, go to an art gallery or museum – somewhere quiet.

Stop watching the news or reading the newspapers.

Unplug the TV. Really. Try it. It helps creativity enormously. And you'll probably find out you suddenly have a lot more free time!

Every day, when you wake up, think of at least three reasons why you're glad to be alive. Try going through the day thinking only happy thoughts! Stop yourself when you feel a dark thought coming on and replace it with a pleasant one. Whatever you do don't think about anything serious.

Now, you're probably thinking I've flipped. How can anybody do this? How could anybody be so carefree when there's so much to worry about?

Well, I don't want to go on about it but, get this, worrying is a choice. You don't have to do it.

I know it's easier said than done. I was there, for almost a decade I worried constantly about my life – where it was heading, whether I was achieving what I should. I grew increasingly depressed about money, debts, my writing, my work, my relationships, everything.

But the trouble with worry is that it actually restricts your ability to perform any of the tasks you're worrying about! It's only when you let go and begin to see yourself in context of the universe - big place, you, an insignificant dot - that you can begin to work out what's important, and what isn't.

On Artistic Temperament

Many talented people, especially artists, musicians, writers and actors are attracted to excitement. The adrenaline buzz.

Look at Hemingway, Scott Fitzgerald, and Dylan Thomas – all chronic alcoholics.

Look at Hendrix, Jim Morrison, Kurt Cobain, Heath Ledger - they all killed themselves, though whether accidentally or not is debatable.

Even some of today's Hollywood actors appear to have similar self-destructive habits.

Excitement, especially ego related, is clearly addictive. When you have tasted life on the edge – or just over it – life can seem dull afterwards. Artists seem to expect their lives should be, if not one long roller coaster, then at least a succession of highs.

Trouble is, instead of channeling those feelings into creativity, they choose other, baser ways of achieving those highs.

This is a shame – especially when it interferes with the talent of the individual.

Thankfully now there is much more help available in this area, and a greater understanding of the issues.

If you think you might have problems, take a good long look at what you do. You might just have an addictive personality that you can channel into other areas.

If you think you have a real problem, you should seek help now, before it's too late. Maybe get some counseling.

More on Artistic Temperament

I've noticed that artistic people are generally more 'sensitive' than others.

This can be good and bad, depending on the maturity of the individual.

It can be good in that a sensitive person will see more of their surroundings, perhaps become more perceptive to details and the nuances of character – a definite boon to a writer.

However, the same sensitivity can make a young ego intolerant of criticism. Temper tantrums are common in this kind of artist.

I'm not saying ego is a bad thing – far from it.

But some people are so sensitive that they feel lashed and beaten by normal life, they feel uncomfortable interacting with others. They're not comfortable without some kind of shield or cloak – like alcohol or drugs.

I think this is the real reason why some apparently talented writers seem to overreact to the slightest of criticism by behaving in a seemingly self-destructive manner.

They don't understand the ego, and what it's for. More on this in the next chapter.

Alcohol

Drinking seems to be common problem amongst writers. It's difficult to know why. Is it writing that drives you to drink, or do drinkers become writers? Is there something about the propensity for self-abuse that is related to creativity? Or does being creative somehow necessitate periods of catatonic stupor?

It's probably none of these things. Perhaps the two are unrelated. Perhaps we're only aware of the problem because, through accident, a significant proportion of the best 'classic' writers have had alcohol problems.

Perhaps it's something to do with forcing the mind open – most writers I've met find the process of thinking through large projects like novels quite draining. Stretching the mind to visualize the enormity of a novel can fill you with a sense of wonder that is as uplifting as it is exhausting. Perhaps alcohol helps to bring you down, back to normal as it were.

But there's more, I think.

Wanting to write a novel, if you think about, is an odd choice to make.

It implies, amongst other things, some dissatisfaction with life, and the way things are.

As if writing fiction can somehow create order and sense for the writer where he or she sees little or none in the real world.

Perhaps it's simply the same dissatisfaction that leads a writer to drink.

My theory is, in the mind of the alcoholic, booze somehow stops time. It arrests consequence and responsibility. Whether they be young, old or any kind of person, a drunk is the same as every other drunk. They all live in the same place, at the same time: nowhere. And alone. It's an almost Zen-like place if you think about it.

Perspective

The whole of this section is about getting a newer, fresher, more balanced view on life.

My experience of writers is that they perform better and are far more productive when they are healthy, happy and clear.

This may surprise you. The traditional image of the struggling artist, angry at the world, is so heavily ingrained into our minds that we almost instinctively wonder why anybody happy would want to write.

For pleasure of course!

Agendas like anger, bitterness and resentment do nothing for your writing, except make you seem at best, obsessed, at worst, crazy.

Writing is about establishing trust. Readers need to know they can relax in your company – that you're not going to disappoint them or be cruel.

Nobody wants to feel insulted. You must not take a reader by the hand only to hit him in the face later on. Agendas show through in your work, unless you edit them furiously when they appear.

Save yourself the tedium of all that work. Get it right first time. How? Easy?

Relax. Get clear. Stay away from harmful activities.

Take in the whole picture, the mature viewpoint.

A reader won't take you seriously as a writer anyway unless you can encompass the whole view. After all, readers think of authors as gods. (Almost!) They are omniscient, all perceiving, omnipotent...

Therefore, it's up to the writer to guide the reader's thoughts to the most important pieces of action and drama for the story. You must never mislead or deceive the reader.

And the only true, easy way to do this is to get healthy – in mind and body.

Reality Bites

Now, I know that you are thinking: Yeah, well, maybe, but that's just not practical at the moment.

Don't put it off. Do it. Start now.

The benefits you reap will be huge.

You can become the writer you want to be. It's a complete fallacy that the most creative writers are miserable individuals who wallow in anguish and self-pity.

Think about it.

Isn't that the definition of an uncreative writer?

If you sincerely want to be creative - get happy!

If you take nothing away from this book but the necessity of learning to be happy, then I will consider myself successful. It's the most important lesson you can learn about life. You have the choice and the right to be happy.

And I believe that happy people attract success.

If you're not happy, it's because you haven't grasped that you – and only you – are the one who's in control of your emotions. Emotions are not designed to make us unhappy - they are there to help us learn.

Learning is good. If you're not learning, you're going nowhere. And if you're staying still, you're stagnating, sinking into obscurity.

It's About Attitude

In order for you to do your best, you must believe that you are doing your best.

Self-doubt, insecurity and lack of confidence are the most common reasons why writers don't write. I've seen it a million times. It's heart breaking.

It's also absurd if you think about it. To become so convinced you couldn't do something well – or at least as well as someone else – that you end up not doing anything!

I've known people who haven't written for a decade because of the fear that what they write will be bad – and they still call themselves writers!

Writers write.

You are not a bad writer because your writing's bad. Think about it. If you know it's bad, you can make it better.

Later, at some stage, you may feel your book will never be any good. This is common.

But how will you ever find out if you don't finish it?

Trust your inner voice – the one that says you want to write. Ignore the doubt, the insecurity, and the lack of confidence. Beat it down, kill it.

The fact is it doesn't matter if you're bad. Even if you think you are, simply ignore those thoughts. Imagine yourself as a successful writer, a creative dynamo. How would you deal with your writing then? Especially if you had a deadline?

You'd have to keep going, wouldn't you? You'd have to. There would be no choice in the matter.

In a short while, perhaps for the first time in your life, you are about to become a real life novel writer. The last thing you want is excess baggage.

Set yourself free.

For the next few days do nothing except unwind, blow away the cobwebs and rejuvenate your spirit!

CHAPTER THREE

Exploding Myths

I'm going to teach you to fly: to write on autopilot.

In order to do that successfully, there's some ground to cover first. There's a lot of what I call wrong thinking that needs to be undone.

You may have written novels before that have taken you a year or two to complete.

This is most probably because you, too, have been a victim of this wrong thinking.

There are myths about writing we all in some way like to perpetuate, perhaps because it makes us feel better about being so unproductive!

The truth is there are far too many myths attached to the business of writing that do absolutely nothing to enhance creativity.

Especially if you believe them.

Before you begin your novel, or next novel, I believe you need to get some of these limiting beliefs out of your mind.

I'm going to spend a little time now trying to dismantle some of these myths for you.

Bear with me. As I mentioned in the introduction, you may not agree with everything I say here. But if, at the very least, you acknowledge that I might be right about a few of these things, I think you'll find your writing becomes a whole lot easier.

Ego

Contrary to what your parents might have told you, your ego is your best friend. I'll tell you why.

Your ego is the motivating force behind your desire to write. It is what makes you want to complete things well, to show them off and be respected for your efforts.

Cherish your ego.

I bet that most of your life you've been taught to suppress your ego. Am I right? It's seen as a raucous child, an inappropriate thing, embarrassing almost. While suppressing a child's ego might make a parent's life easier, it is not necessarily a good thing to suppress it in a writer.

The ego is fragile. It should be nurtured like a delicate plant that you must water, protect and treat with respect.

But here's the trick.

Don't share it. Direct it inward.

Imagine it growing inside you, expanding, filling you with pride and the belief that you can do anything. The ego is not logical. It has no sense of the impossible.

Whenever you catch yourself filling with pride or beginning to feel that anything and everything is possible – go with it, push the feeling to the limit. Imagine that you really are the most talented and best, cleverest, superb writer you know.

Even if it seems absurd, keep telling yourself you're the best. Make yourself laugh with the absurdity of it.

Why?

Because your subconscious will start to believe it. Basically, in terms of intellect, the subconscious is stupid – it believes whatever you tell it. If that is case, surely you have a responsibility to tell it only positive things.

For complex reasons, the subconscious remembers things even better when they're attached to emotion. A burst of ego-driven thoughts and the associated rush of adrenaline are like radiation burns to the subconscious – permanently imprinting good, helpful pictures on your inner being. Within a short time, your self-worth will start to soar as your subconscious begins to believe in the endless possibilities that your ego is capable of imagining. Go with it. Enjoy it.

Okay, I know you're thinking this is all self-delusion. How is this helping my writing?

So, for those that haven't got the central message of this book, I'll state it again:

You can write a brilliant novel, simply if you believe you can.

And it will be as easy as you want it to be because you decide that it will be.

Keep it to Yourself

One of the ways of sustaining this new level of confidence in yourself is not to share your newfound feelings with anyone.

There are other reasons for this that I will explain later. For the moment we'll just deal with some home truths.

People love to criticize. It's part of human nature.

Walk into a room and tell someone you're happy and the natural instinct is for the other person to tell you why you shouldn't be.

People will always try to undermine your confidence – especially if it's seen to be ego driven. People think that if your ego is telling you something, you are being fed false information and should be brought down to earth immediately.

Why is that?

Doers, especially creative doers, intimidate people. Let's face it; non-doers are intimidated because they're jealous. It's not worth talking to these people. Rather than waste your energy telling people how good you feel, don't bother. Because their next question will always be, Why? Or, What makes you so special?

To which your answer will be, naturally, Because I'm such a great writer!

I'll leave it to you to imagine the response you'll get from that one.

The lesson is that the ego is a private thing.

Don't tell anyone else about your opinion about yourself – however short-lived because others will always try to undermine your confidence. It's human nature.

To recap, your ego is good because it's your motivating force.

Think about what your ego thrives on:

* *Attention*
* *Recognition*
* *Praise*
* *Flattery – no matter how empty!*

All of the things that will make you feel better about yourself and your writing.

Of course the ego is shallow, capricious and child-like. That's a given -accepted. But its energy knows no bounds. It is blindly convinced it can do anything. Therefore it is powerful. It's up to you to harness the energy it thrives on and make it work for you.

The rational, and the logical, conscious mind must be forced back to let the subconscious come forward. The subconscious will then be able to take over and do all the hard work for you.

The hardest part is simply to trust it and not feel you're deluding yourself. You're not.

You're simply bolstering your confidence to powerful, super creative levels.

Don't fear your ego. Promote it, protect it and make it grow!

Nay Sayers

Many people will tell you that this kind of ego bolstering is a bad thing. These people are usually small minded, cynical and depressed, but you might be tempted to listen to them anyway. It's hard not to – they're everywhere!

They'll say you shouldn't elevate your opinion of yourself to impossible heights, that it's not logical or realistic.

That's because people associate egos with arrogance and unpleasantness. They imagine prima donnas who stamp their feet and scream if they don't get their own way. True, the ego can make you behave like that –but it doesn't have to.

There is another way. An ego that shows itself through quiet confidence, and an easy, giving manner.

Look at some actors or athletes. Just after a good performance, they are filled with their own egos, brimming with confidence, happy.

But also note there is rarely any bitterness or anger. There is serenity, surety and confidence.

This is how you must think of ego. Strong and benevolent.

Ego is a pre-requisite to creativity.

Think about it. Without ego, there would be no urge for humans to do anything beyond survive. The ego is what makes us human, what makes us scale new heights. It is what takes us out of ourselves, gives us the courage to travel the world, or the strength to rebel against our enemies – the need to prove something to ourselves, to stand tall and say: I did that!

Some might say: what about altruism? What about the desire to give and do good just because it's the right thing to do. Pah! There's no such thing as altruism. People give because it feels good – to them. Altruism is just ego in another form.

Don't fear your ego, and don't let anyone take it away from you.

It's who you are, and who you can become.

Motivation

So now you've got a motivating force – your ego, what are you going to do with it?

Let's ask some basic questions. It might help at this stage.

* *Why do you want to write?*
* *In particular, why do you want to write a novel?*

Answer in less than 25 words – the fewer the better.

Answering this question is important. It may well define how you go about reading the rest of this book, and how much you derive from it.

Most professionals will answer in just a few words.

* *I can't help it.*
* *I've got this great story.*
* *I have a deadline.*

These are the answers of well-motivated people, and even their answers sound woolly!

Think for a moment. There is absolutely no reason in the world for the average person to write a novel. What's the point? A lot of effort for what? A whole bunch of words that perhaps only a few people will ever read.

Put like that, it doesn't seem worth the effort, does it?

The great Dorothea Brande once said, "Writers create their own sense of emergency."

She's right.

It's weird. For some reason writers decide that it is critical that they write.

Why? Who knows? Why does it seem so important for a writer that he writes?

I guess it's about creativity. Once you've felt the satisfaction that comes with creating something – especially when you receive positive feedback - it quickly becomes as addictive as a drug. This is an ego related thing, obviously. Writing is about creating.

Words, pictures, scenes, worlds, whatever.

Perhaps there's even something a little god-like about being able to create things, to fashion raw, chaotic nature into something beautiful and meaningful.

What about your reasons to write?

If you are not a professional you will probably have much more practical reasons for writing a novel. For instance:

* To record a family history
* To relate a dramatic event in your life
* To get that plot that's been bugging you for years down on paper
* To prove that you can do it

All good solid reasons. The fact is, any and all reasons to write a novel are valid, as long as they achieve the desired end-result.

For now, I want you write down the reasons why you want to write a novel, or novels.

Do it now. It's kind of a test.

The Three Keys

There are three simple keys to writing a novel quickly and easily. They have nothing to do with anything you might have learned at school.

They've got nothing to do with grammar, spelling, composition, knowing the rules – these are all to do with the craft of writing – and the subject of the second half of the book. Easy stuff, you can learn in a day.

I'm talking about the art of writing a novel.

Here are the three keys:

* *Attitude*
* *Mindset*
* *Courage*

That's it. With these keys, you can unlock the doors to endless creativity, boundless motivation and effortless work.

Hopefully by now, you'll be getting a clearer idea of how to create a positive attitude in yourself – and how to use your ego to help you unleash the power of it.

Next chapter we'll be dealing with mindset in detail – and how changing your views on things can help you to break out of the limiting belief systems that prevent writers from writing quickly and easily.

Courage is important too, because in the final stretch, you'll need to take a leap of faith.

A whole novel might seem like an awesome prospect – even at the end of this book.

However, it is my sincere desire that by the time you finish reading – and probably a long time before that – if you follow the rules and techniques I'm teaching you, you'll be so desperate to get started, you'll wonder what ever held you back!

Part of the process is demystifying the business of creative writing.

The fact is, too many people don't write, or don't even try, because they think it's too hard. And the worse thing? Writers perpetuate the myth!

Of course they do!

Think about it – they have to. How much respect would the ordinary person have for writers if they thought writing was easy?

For that matter, how much respect would writers have for themselves?

Everyone loves the image of the struggling artist in his garret, where he sits wrapped in his old coat and scarf against the cold. Where each word is wrenched from his heart and spills on to the page like blood. He's alone, frustrated, a misunderstood genius. The whole image is romantic. It's noble. It's…

It's garbage!

To my mind, anyone who struggles to write simply isn't doing it right!

I've seen writers struggle for years over all kinds of things:

* *They're waiting for Inspiration*
* *They're wracked with doubt*
* *They're avoiding confronting their work (or themselves)*
* *They whine about lack of time*

The list goes on.

The interesting part is that, when writers become fully engrossed in their novel, all of these concerns evaporate.

Suddenly inspiration is there, banging on the door, begging to be heard. Doubt disappears and they just seem to be able to make the time they never had before.

It's looking at this seemingly contradictory behavior, and trying to make sense of it that, in large part, has led to this book.

There's no big secret to writing a novel.

Rather it's a sequence of events. Not just physical events but also moments of decision that a writer must go through to reach the endpoint of "novelist". Some writers take years to learn the knack of it.

The object of this book it to help you through those events and moments of decision in the shortest time possible.

They say there's a book in everyone. Simply put, I want to bring one out of you.

Why? Because I've always loved helping people. Especially helping people to become creative, helping them find that spark of creativity that sets us apart from the rest of nature.

I love seeing the sense of pride and well being that shines from people that are creative and loving it. It's awesome and inspiring.

At moments, the satisfaction that creativity can bring you is overwhelming. It's almost like being a god. Indeed, if you think about it, that's exactly what you are when you're writing… a kind of mini-god, co-creating the universe.

Birth of an Idea

Writing a novel is like having a baby.

It's great fun to conceive. It's exciting when you know it's on the way. Its actual birth may be beautiful or it may be traumatic, it may be quick and painless or long drawn out and stressful. But when it's arrived, it's so wonderful it fills you with aching pride – but with it comes responsibility.

Writing a book makes you feel special. I guarantee that when you've finished your magnum opus, you'll feel much better about yourself – not only because you'll be an author but also because you'll know you can finish things. You'll know that anything is possible and that any of your lifelong ambitions can be fulfilled.

But first, we need to look at your thinking and perhaps change a few of your long held beliefs...

ROB PARNELL

CHAPTER FOUR

A Case of Definition

The purpose of this series of observations is to break down barriers to creativity and output. If you take on board the ideas I'm about to propound, even for a short while, you'll find your productivity will soar.

And as we know, writers get better in direct proportion to their productivity.

Okay, let's start with the big issues first.

What is Art?

What would be your definition?

A beautiful, well executed piece of sculpture? A piece of music so divinely inspired that it seems almost holy? A painting so sublime that it seems to ring of truth itself?

What about art in literary terms?

Is it writing so clever and profound you are humbled – even intimidated - by every word?

It may be any of these things.

It may be none of them.

Who's to say that one piece of creativity is art and another is not? Who is the arbiter?

Is it you? Me? Some unnamed critic who seems to speak with authority?

Given time, people seem to agree that certain items become Art, while some don't.

Michelangelo's David. Leonardo's Mona Lisa, Beethoven's 5th Symphony, Guernica by Picasso. All these are agreed by most to be Works of Art.

There are others who might disagree.

What is all this telling you? That "art" is merely a consensus of opinion?

Yes, that's exactly what it is. No more or less. Nothing can be called true "art" without agreement between people.

Art is not an absolute. It is subjective. Get that fixed in your mind.

What is art today is trash tomorrow, and vice versa.

There is absolutely no reason to believe that what you create is less a 'work of art' than anything else.

Look at pieces of pottery from pre-history. They are rare, beautiful and stirring. Some call them examples of primitive art. In their own time they may well have been mass-produced in thousands, badly tooled, thought of as merely functional, cheap and thrown away after use!

Imagine that in a thousand years the world has been destroyed. Aliens land on our wasted planet and by chance find your book. Everyone else's has gone for some reason. Do you think your book would then become a work of art to these aliens? You can be damn sure it would. Errors and all.

It's all relative.

What really makes art?

One word: Rarity.

The reason why David and the Mona Lisa are considered exceptional works of art is because they are one in a million. They represent supposed perfection in their field.

Everything else that might be a bit like them is conveniently classed as inferior and relegated to an also subjective realm of "second-class" art. An absurd concept, for a start.

Does that mean other artists never produce anything worthy of praise? Of course not.

How many pieces of art do you know that have stirred you and had a profound effect on you, only to discover later that some critic has relegated the work to banal and uninspiring?

Art is what you perceive it to be. If you believe your book to be a work of art, then that's exactly what it is. Period.

There is absolutely no reason why you should not consider yourself an Artist – with a capital A!

You do not need to pass exams to call yourself an artist. You are an artist because you decide to be - not because you necessarily create art, but because you aspire to be an artist.

Remember - writing is not art in itself. Writing can create a work of art, yes, but the act of writing and writing well is a craft.

And a craft is a learned set of rules that you adapt to express yourself.

Just like Michelangelo, Leonardo, Beethoven and Picasso. They all learned the rules of their craft first – and just kept going. Each one of them labored and produced until one day, perhaps by chance, they created a piece of work that later generations would regard as a work of real art.

Artists do not always set out to create art. Mostly they set out to express themselves in the best way they can. Whether they succeed every time is open to question and analysis.

It's like swimming.

If you swim badly, you sink. If you swim well, you get stronger and go further. The fact is, the only way to improve your swimming is to swim.

Swimmers swim.

Writers write. That's the only way to get better. If you keep going, one day you too will create your masterpiece. Your work of art.

It's practically inevitable!

What is Originality?

There's a lot of nonsense talked about originality, especially by critics, students and teachers. The media doesn't help either.

Publishers, TV and film companies are always talking about it. If you read their guidelines for submissions, they practically insist on it – every time!

If you're an avid reader or TV and movie watcher, you may think this odd. Because if originality is so important to producers and publishers, why do we never see or read anything that appears remotely original anymore?

When was the last time you saw an 'original' film, or read an 'original' book?

Hmm? Me neither.

Perhaps our definition is faulty. Perhaps it's different from what these media moguls regard as original.

Or is it that they themselves are using the wrong word?

They don't really mean original. They mean significantly different – that is, the same old thing with a new twist. Which, as any seasoned professional will tell you, is not actually being original at all!

Originality is a very scary word for a young artist. I've met several writers that spend valuable writing time too terrified to write lest they be considered unoriginal. They desperately try to think of an 'original' idea, as though this is a key that will unlock the door to their creativity and success.

What a waste of time!

There is no such thing as an original idea.

There might be interesting juxtapositions of old ideas but even these aren't really worth seeking out. Someone will always get there before you. Don't waste your time, please.

Trouble is, critics (especially) believe that true originality is something that is quantifiable and exists in a recognizable form – and that it's the sole preserve of a few selected geniuses – which strangely enough, only they are qualified to recognize.

Inspiration is a gift, yes, but the truth is it's as common a commodity as water, if you know how to recognize it.

Think about it – there are only so many words, only so many formats, only so many plots, only so many ways to string together a sentence, a scene, a drama, or a story. In reality, there are precious few ideas and concepts worth exploring – all of which have been done to death a million times before you were born. How in hell can you hope to be original?

The simple answer is that you can't.

Don't even try - because it will stifle you until you can't do a thing!

Originality in Publishing

You may think you have an original concept. Quite apart from this being an impossibility by definition, sometimes an idea comes along that – in the context of the time – will seem relatively original.

Be assured, it won't stay original for long. There's a curious phenomenon that publishers will tell about if you ask them. When they come across an 'original' idea submitted by a writer, within days - or sometimes minutes - about a dozen or so other writers seem to have had the same idea at about the same time. All submitted independently of each other.

Curious, eh?

Without getting too metaphysical, this is a difficult phenomenon to explain. Do original ideas float about in the ether waiting to be picked up by receptive artists? I doubt it.

I think it's because we're all watching the same news items, reading the same papers, making the same mental connections that lead us to certain conclusions, or inspiring us in certain ways that are common.

If you think about it, that means for every good idea you have, the unfortunate fact is there is bound to be someone else out there having exactly the same idea – at exactly the same time as you are. What a depressing thought.

I guess one way to stop this from happening is to "cut yourself off". That way, your ideas percolate, undiluted and untainted. The longer you hold on to a series of thoughts and develop them in your mind, the more chance the end result will be something that only you could have thought of – therefore, more likely to be considered original.

Unique Voice

To look for originality is to misunderstand it. My feeling is that true originality will most likely come from someone who doesn't realize they have it.

Writing teachers are always trying to get us to emulate success. They want us to copy others, so that we might learn – and then we wonder why we're not seen as original!

Originality, if it's anywhere, is in our own voice.

Everyone has a different way of looking at something and a way of expressing a reaction to it. It is well attested that ten people witnessing the same event will report ten different versions of it. This is not because they see different things. No. It's because they describe it to themselves in ten different ways.

We are unique in the way that each of us experiences the world.

That is what makes us original.

Get the following fact firmly established in your mind:

Originality is nothing more than a combination of honesty and attitude. Good writers know this and strive to achieve both of these to the best of his or her ability in their writing.

If you want to be original – be yourself. That is the only rule.

It's up to others less talented and less focused – and always has been – to define originality. Don't get involved with their trite definitions.

Artists should be above petty, meaningless labels.

What is Inspiration?

The feeling that something is right. It's that sense of elation you feel at some new insight.

Hence: inspiration is not the idea itself, but the way it makes you feel. And the way you feel is what makes you unique. Here, we're getting closer to a better definition of originality. If we combine inspiration with honesty, we are getting closer to a mindset that can create great art.

If you are totally honest and true to your beliefs in your writing, then what you create will be truly unique. And only by being unique can you claim to be original. After all, there's only one you.

Audiences, readers, and viewers like honesty, no matter how lurid or bland - they expect and admire it. By the same token, if your work is failing, try asking yourself - do I really believe in my characters, my plots, or my stories? Or am I just playing games - trying to be clever? Chances are, if you don't believe in what you do, neither will anyone else.

Some people wait their entire lives for inspiration, believing that it is some innate outside influence that will one day hit them, along with the motivation to do something about it.

Wrong.

Inspiration comes from within.

With the right mindset, inspiration – that is: good ideas – are all around you, jostling for position, eager for your attention. Indeed, there are so many thousands of inspiring ideas close at hand that you simply don't recognize them as such.

Until you train yourself to see them.

Here's one of my favorite exercises:

How to Come Up With Ten Ideas for Stories before Breakfast

Ideas that inspire are usually caused by a juxtaposition of one notion against another seemingly unrelated one. That's one definition. In reality, it's anything that causes your mind to take a step back and say: "Now, that's interesting."

Take a good look at the following scenarios and see if they don't suggest stories to you:

1. You wake up in the morning in your bed. Imagine you've woken up in a bed you don't recognize. Why are you here? What happened...?

2. You get out of bed, your own bed this time. The floor has blood on it...

3. You step from the bed towards the bathroom. You hear a sound and look back. With a shock, you see yourself – you're still asleep in bed...

4. You make it to the bathroom and look in the mirror. It's not your face...

5. You bathe. You can't remember last night at all...

6. You put on some clothes, there's a pendant in a pocket you don't recognize...

7. You walk downstairs and pick up the post. There's a letter from a lawyer...

8. You open the fridge. Someone – God knows who – has moved your stuff around.

9. You put on the kettle. You hear ticking from a package on the table...

10. You put on the toaster. It turns into a frog...

You get the idea?

There is absolutely nothing that happens to us, or anything we can imagine that cannot be seen as a starting point for an interesting idea.

Contrary to what most of us believe, inspiration is one of those things that can be forced. Professional writers know this.

If you're ever stuck for an idea, the best way to think of something is to try your own version of the above exercise. Tell yourself you're going to think of ten ideas – and you will.

For some reason the subconscious mind likes this kind of exercise and will deliver you more and more wild ideas the longer you seek them.

Try it. I guarantee it always works!

Inspiration is cheap and plentiful. Remember that.

What is Literacy?

A quick look back over best sellers from the past thirty years will tell you that literacy is not a particular issue when it comes to popular writers.

It's not really my place to bandy names of authors with less than "ideal" literary skills – just take my word for it. It's not important.

Of course, there are a few rules that we must abide by nowadays – and I list them all in Parts Two and Three of the book. Just don't knock yourself out about them.

Publishers are quick to say they reject illiterate manuscripts. I would be ready to believe them if they didn't publish so many.

I think perhaps the problem is that publishers, even editors, aren't quite as well educated as they'd like us to believe. They're just like you and me. If they like a story, they'll go with it. If it's patchy, no matter. If it's terrible, they'll pay someone to "fix it up". It happens all too often.

Perhaps there's a more romantic reason. Perhaps ours is such a rich culture, there is room for all kinds of writing styles, however crude and undisciplined.

Just a theory.

What is Genius?

There's a lot of disagreement about this. Again. I would like to put forward my view, not as the definitive answer but one that is more helpful to you, the creator, trying to forge an easier way through your writing.

Begin by removing all your preconceptions.

Genius is not an innate substance that only the lucky few possess.

Again, as with art, it is a value judgment ascribed to an artist after his work has been completed. Nobody is a genius before he/she has created something. How could he/she be – without something to judge them by?

Scott Adams – of Dilbert fame – once said that genius is the ability to effectively disguise your influences. If you do that, he argued, you can "con" people into believing you have presented something original – ah, that word again.

I like this definition, but it does sound too simple.

When asked how he could come up with the Theory of Relativity, Einstein said he simply imagined himself sat on a point of light. And worked backwards.

Is this the mark of a genius? Someone who can think outside of the square? To be able to imagine a concept that no one else had previously considered? At the time when Einstein was thinking these thoughts, most scientists believed light traveled through an "ether" rather like a dye through water. Einstein realized this couldn't be the case because light could be "bent" by gravity. In the face of all scientific thinking, he proposed that light was a form of energy – and that he could prove it by math.

Did this make him a genius? Or was it just a desire not to believe what the herd had been told?

I think that's partly it. Even so, Einstein is still only perceived as a genius in retrospect.

At school, he was apparently considered an average student, inattentive and destined for obscurity.

Some say Edison was a genius because he never gave up inventing. Similarly, Mozart is considered a genius because he found composing so easy.

All of these people just did what they had to. They didn't think: Today I'm going to be a genius...

I think people label someone a genius as a kind of excuse. It makes their talent seem unattainable. People would rather not believe that each one of us is capable of genius.

The point is that genius is generally indefinable, most especially by the people who bandy the term around.

It's just a handy way of describing talent that doesn't seem to rely on exterior elements. Something that comes from within.

People make this judgment because genii are not only defined by the work they create but also by the way they go about it. Their personal style, as it were.

What is Style?

In writing, it's the one thing that all writers have – before critics, teachers and peers try to beat it out of you! This is a mistake because our unformed 'style' is potentially the very essence of our genius.

As I say, everyone has a unique voice.

Every writer has a different way of saying the same thing – a unique way. Journalism tries to block this voice – it's too personal and inappropriate for news. In fiction, it is essential. Take away an author's unique voice and you have only imitation – work that is shallow and does not inspire.

Therefore, in fiction, you must believe that your own unique voice is as valid as anyone else's.

Your unique voice is what separates you from everyone else. Don't let anyone take it away from you!

Yes, study and learn the techniques of the craft of writing, by all means, but when it comes to writing fiction, tell it your way with your own unique point of view.

You have it. We all have it. We all have our own way of seeing the world.

It is a strange phenomenon that a writer's first book will often sell better than any of the later ones. Why is that?

Because readers recognize a new, unique voice. Readers like getting inside a new writer's head. Especially if they can relate to him or her. Even more if they can relate to them and want to do and say the things the reader wouldn't dare.

My advice is, at all times in fiction, to be true to your own voice, your own convictions and your own view of the world, no matter what. Then, your style will shine.

What is Talent?

The only right way to tell a story is in your own words.

This sounds obvious but to the novice, this is not always as easy as it sounds.

When you ask people to write something, they tend to go into writing mode – something they picked up from school – whereby there are certain words and phrases you must use to be doing it right.

Big mistake. Nothing is more likely to sound wooden and contrived.

If you're having trouble finding your voice, try this little experiment.

First, write down a couple or five lines telling a very short story. Like an anecdote. If you can't think of anything, try relating the plot of a movie or a book. It'll read something like this:

My brother was once taught an important lesson about taking on more than he could handle. When he was younger, he used to go fishing. One day, he was pulled into the water by a large fish. He was soaked to the skin and had to be hospitalized.

Pretty dull, eh?

Now try telling the story out loud – preferably into a tape recorder. Tell the story, as if you have an audience of one or more friends.

When you listen back to it, it'll probably sound a bit like this:

Hey, wanna hear something funny? Yeah – um – well, you know my brother? Jack, yeah. The one with the funny hair, yeah. Well, um, y'know, he was always a bit of an idiot. He always reckoned he could do anything, right? Y'know, kind of like a dare devil, never say die kind of guy. An idiot, yeah right. So anyway, he was out fishing one day. In a boat on this loch, up in Scotland I think it was. Um... so anyway. He got this big fish and it kept pulling the line out. Every time he tried to pull it in, the fish – whatever it was – kept pulling harder. Huh, yeah, I know, it's typical of him, I know. So anyway, he stood up and the thing reared out of the water – it was a huge monster he said – and it pulled him in. Right over the side of the boat, into the water. Wham. Um, yeah, okay? Splash! Finally pulled himself out and walked back to the house. Idiot got the flu didn't he? We took him to hospital. Spent about a week there... I visited him all the time. What an idiot.

You'll notice it's a lot longer, almost incoherent in places but also full of tiny details.

Not just actual physical details but details in the nuance of its telling that actually add weight to the tale. You learn more about the event because of the way it's told. You also learn not only about the hero, but also the teller, because the story is now influenced by his personality.

Now, rewrite the tape-recorded transcript, editing out all the ums and glitches and polishing the prose slightly. It might read something like this:

My brother Jack: he's the one with the funny hair.

He was sometimes an idiot. He reckoned he could do just about anything. To be fair, he was a dare devil, a never-say-die kind of guy.

Anyway, Jack was out fishing one day, in a boat on a loch, up in Scotland. His line caught a big fish, but he couldn't reel it in.

Every time Jack pulled, the fish kept pulling harder. Jack stood up. Just then, a monstrous creature reared up out of the water. Jack was so stunned, he lost his balance. The monster-fish pulled him in, right over the side of the boat.

Splash!

Quickly, afraid for his life, he scrabbled back to the boat and hauled himself out of the water. Later, we took him to the hospital because, after that, he got the flu. Poor Jack.

You see the difference? You may not have a literary masterpiece but you do have something that's alive, exciting and more importantly, believable.

The Difference between Fact and Fiction

Fact, by definition, is what actually happened.

However incredible the events, a journalist's job is to report facts. They may be startling, bland, incredible or dull. It doesn't matter. Journalists are taught to keep themselves out of the writing – to not even call attention to the fact there's a remote observer – and tell exactly what happened. Of course, total objectivity is almost impossible. Writing is always tainted by some external influence whether it is editorial policy or public perception. But that's how facts must come across – as a true representation of what actually happened.

Fiction is different. No matter how incredible or dull, fiction has to be believable.

One of the great rules of fiction is that EVEN IF what you're writing ACTUALLY happened, it is not good fiction if it's not believable.

Think about that for a moment. When you ponder the implications of that sentence, you realize what you are up against.

Fiction has its own rules. Readers aren't interested in the "truth"; they're interested in what is believable – which are completely different animals. Even if you write about monsters and demons or aliens, as long as your story is believable, in a sense it is more TRUE than fact.

How often have you heard people say that something real would make a great story?

And how often do you hear the counter: But no one would ever believe it!

This is great, it gives you a huge range to play with.

Don't fall into the trap of writing the truth just because it actually happened. If the reader doesn't believe it, it might as well not have happened. If it doesn't work, it's just bad fiction.

In writing groups this happens all the time. The young writer tells of some horrendous event in their lives. The other writers say they didn't believe the main character's plight – it wasn't credible.

The young writer is outraged and squeals, But that's what happened! It doesn't matter.

If you really want to get across the real horror of what happened, you will probably have to completely fictionalize the whole event – changing all the facts and motivations of the characters to even get close to making it seem real.

Ironic, don't you think?

Conclusion

I hope that by now you're beginning to see that real writing has got very little to do with what other people think. It's got absolutely nothing to do with other people's value judgments. I hope that from this chapter you've begun to understand that what other people think of your writing is irrelevant. Especially when you're starting out.

The best writers are those that keep going no matter how bad they might seem at first.

Conversely, being a naturally good speller or grammarian, for instance, doesn't guarantee that you'll have any of the qualities necessary to become a good, prolific author.

If nothing else, I hope you're beginning to realize that, in today's world, writing success often requires a lot more dedication than talent.

CHAPTER FIVE

Defeating the Enemy

Now we're going to deal with some practical elements that might help you during your writing, especially if you're going to sit down and write a novel in a month. Indeed, there are tips here that will last you a lifetime!

Lack of Time

This is probably the single most consistent complaint you hear from writers, especially beginners.

What's interesting is that writers who really want to write seem to be able to make the time their peers have so much trouble finding!

It's about commitment – but not always. Let's just run through a few of the problems you might encounter and suggest ways of dealing with them:

The seven most common barriers to finding writing time:

* *Your day job*
* *Domestic chores*

* Friends / other social commitments
* Family, spouses, children, relatives, & their commitments
* TV, Internet, Computer games
* Concentration – dealing with distractions
* Sports – watching or competing

I would guess that all of the above have at some time got in the way of your writing and especially the important task of writing a novel. The trouble is, if you let them, these things will get in the way of anything you ever want to do!

There again, most people spend decades, if not their entire lives, being distracted from the important things and leave this planet no better off than they found it.

That's the nature of being human, to an extent.

But in the writer's life, there must come a time when you say, No, this is not enough for me - I have to write that book!

Bearing in mind that you must allocate time – not too long but ideally every day - the following advice may help. You have no choice. If you sincerely want to write, you will have to deal with each of the barriers one at a time. Take some time out now to analyze how you spend your time and work out why these things are so time-consuming.

The Day Job

This is an obvious time destroyer if you want to take yourself seriously as a writer. Seven, eight, nine, ten or more hours of "prime" writing time wasted every single day! Just think what you could achieve in that time!

It can be frustrating, sure – especially if you hate your day job. The fact is though, you need to pay the rent and the bills. If you're feeling stuck and wish you had more time, don't despair.

Taking sick days off to write is not a great solution. Mainly because inconsistent bursts of creativity can be counter-productive. What you're looking for is a routine. It's regularity that is the key. You should be writing every day if you can, even if it's only for an hour or two. The brain seems to prefer this approach.

If you write once a week for instance, you'll probably spend half an hour or so just getting into the right mood to write – obviously a waste of your time. You need to get into a productive rhythm as soon as possible to maximize the use of your time. Writing every day helps here – shortening this "adjustment" time down considerably.

The trick is to put aside time. Take it forcibly if you have to!

Lunchtime.
There's a whole hour you could be writing.

Before work.
Perhaps before anyone else in the house gets up. One hour - from six till seven.

After work.
Perhaps you could stop off in a café or bar on the way home. Just for an hour or so – so that it doesn't impact too greatly on your home life, if that's an issue for you.

Perhaps you're lucky and can write consistently during the evenings. If you're young and unattached, you might be able to write for three or four hours at a stretch!

Most of us, though, have family commitments that make being unsociable every evening a sure way to annoy everyone in the house!

There's always the writer's favorite: Late at night, when everyone else is in bed. It's probably not the best time to write - when you're tired at the end of the day. But many of us do it because it's the only time available.

Just don't stay up too late – or it will impact on the following day!

In the past I tried all of these ways to write whilst having a day job - as have many writers before. Now that I haven't had a 'proper' job for over a decade, I can say without question that if you want to be a career writer you MUST start arranging your life so that the writing comes first. Even when you have a day job.

I was eventually sacked from my last job (back in 2002) because everyone in the office knew my writing was more important than my job. My boss explained she thought she was doing me a favor when she terminated my contract. And to be honest, she did.

Domestic Chores

These can be good for you!

Rather than trying to get out of household chores, you should welcome them. There's something about repetitive physical work that can liberate the mind. Every time you're chained to the sink or cleaning floors or ironing, use the time to reflect on your work.

Chances are, as soon as you're finished, you'll be heading for that word processor!

Friends

It's very easy – too easy – to become so involved with friends and their often time-consuming issues that you never have any time left to write.

The fact is, if you're hopelessly gregarious and can't bear to be alone, you might not have the right temperament to be a writer. However, this is not carved in stone. I've known several writers who are very sociable but who manage to find the time to write well – and quickly.

It's easy enough to put off friends for a while if you need to get some writing done. All manner of excuses will work. Laundry, hair washing, bad cold, DIY needs doing. You could even tell the truth. You want some time to write!

However, others are not so easily put off...

Family

Count yourself lucky if you're single! Writers with spouses and children will tell you of the endless battles that ensue for their time. It doesn't matter that your family want you to stand around like a lemon, being totally unproductive. They just want you there.

Anything less is a betrayal!

Unless you have very supportive family members, the fact is you'll probably never be able to totally please a spouse or child. My experience is that non-writers often regard writing as a frivolous activity, not to be encouraged.

That's why it's doubly important that you negotiate with the people around you. If they won't give you the time you want, then ask them when they would prefer you to take the time.

If they dismissively suggest the middle of the night, suggest in that case you might need to sleep in for longer. I know I'm painting a dark picture. Perhaps it won't be as tough for you. For me, over the course of many relationships, it was always hard - until I met Robyn, my wife, also a writer, who finally understood!

If it is tough for you – and it can be for many fledgling writers - you have to keep pressing, letting the people around you know just how important this is to you. Most people will be reasonable. You may have a partner who is not. I know, I had several.

Everyone has seen the dedications in the front of books to partners. Writers are the first to acknowledge that it is the support of the partner that is critical to writing success. Without that, you may be forced to give up, move on or end up miserable about not being "allowed" to write.

I have dedicated the whole of the following section to this problem, as I believe it is more common that most writers would like to admit.

Partners

For some reason, those closest to you probably don't want you to write. Even if they do, or appear to, they don't want you to be a success.

Why is this? How can this be?

Because it rocks the boat. It changes the status quo.

Writing is a mysterious activity. One moment you are alone for hours on end, the next you're getting notice and respect from outsiders to the relationship. This can be an uncomfortable experience for partners who've grown used to the way things are/were and don't share your need to, as they see it, 'change things.'

How many times have writers heard the following words?

When you're rich and famous you'll:

* *Leave me*
* *Won't want to be with me*
* *Get a beautiful / handsome new partner*

Of course, all of these worries are mostly absurd and not something that the writer is even considering. Nonetheless, some partners seem to equate success with altering of circumstances, as though we writers only tolerate our lives the way they are because we're not rich and famous!

I think the problem is that when writers take the time to explain to their partners that they need to write, the spouse assumes you're not happy and that you really want to change some things about your life and in particular the relationship.

This reaction has more to do with the insecurity of the partner that it does about anything else.

The spouse may assume that your need to write suggests that they're not fulfilling you or that it's really your spouse that you're dissatisfied with!

You should tread carefully in this area because it is important. Reassurances may be necessary: promises of commitment, fidelity etc. Whatever. Compromise a little if you have to but do not be distracted from the main aim – to get some writing time!

Children also, will probably not understand. But no matter how guilty you feel, you have to be strong if writing is important to you.

Children are naturally selfish – they have to be, to survive. They also take great delight in wasting time doing nothing more than 'being with you.' Understandable when they're very young. But once they're old enough to understand, it's your turn to be selfish! Take that time. Get in a friend to baby-sit if you have to!

If there's absolutely no way you can get the time at home – and it happens that way sometimes – steal it.

There are plenty of places to slink away to:

* *Cafes*
* *Bars*
* *Libraries*
* *Parks*
* *The beach*
* *A secluded spot in the hills!*

If all else fails, visit a friend and ask if you can "borrow" a room for a while – an hour or two a day preferably.

Just get some alone time. The fact is, even if you never write a book, your sanity will benefit from this time. Especially if it is so hard won!

If your spouse or your family inquire as to your new absences, tell them it's what you've been forced to do – by their attitude. Eventually they'll have to see how important the issue is for you.

Other Distractions

By far the biggest time wasters though are ones we force on ourselves. TV is the bane of our lives. I have one piece of advice in this area. Destroy. Get rid of the one eyed monster! It'll change your life – for the better. Suddenly there will be a vast gulf of spare time you never realized you had. Who knows – you might not even miss it!

Same goes for computer games. Hide them. Uninstall them from your computer. Stop putting temptation in your way.

Think twice before you go on to the Internet again. It too is a huge time waster!

I know some people say that writers must communicate with their readers. That they absolutely must do some of the necessary social marketing! But this is really not true.

There are many professional writers out there doing fine, who NEVER engage in social marketing. They say they'd rather be writing...

Now – back to issues concerning the craft...

On Sharing your Work

As a way to placate your loved ones, you may feel tempted to show them your writing - or even just talk about it.

This is generally an humungous mistake.

The message here is a simple one: Unless, it's finished, don't.

Think of your writing as a fine wine or homebrew. While you're working on something, it's bubbling inside the vat of your mind. It's maturing, gaining strength.

Your imagination is the sugar and yeast that you add. The brewing process takes time – your ideas need to ferment. And everybody knows the worst thing you can do to a fine wine or beer is to open the top and let in some air.

It's the same with writing.

Telling in person dissipates the need to tell in writing.

The great ghost story writer MR James noted this and stopped telling his stories to his pupils, though they begged him to. He realized that if you tell your story first, the subconscious mind is satisfied the story is out – and doesn't feel so compelled to write it down.

Repeat: Keep it to yourself

There are other reasons for this.

You may feel proud of something you've just written and want to show it off. The trouble is any comment - good or bad - will needle away at you and your ego. You must not let this happen. It's very important that you and only you act as the judge and arbiter of your work until it's finished.

Criticism will distract you from your goal. Other people's comments may inspire you but will also distract you from your purpose. Even positive comments are bad – they can make you concentrate on the wrong aspects of your story. The point is, it doesn't matter what other people think until they see the whole manuscript. Until then, consider your stuff unreadable!

Also, remember this:

The very worst person to show your writing to is your partner or to a close family member!

Why?

Think about it. There are only three reactions a well meaning partner can come up with:

It's really good

It's terrible

It's not bad.

Good, bad or indifferent, each comment is death to your creativity!

Your mind will go into mental somersaults trying to interpret the comments. Like these:

If it's really good, how come they didn't notice the bad bits?

If it's so terrible why should I bother?

If I don't think it's bad, why do they? What else are they trying to say? Is it really bad and I can't see it? Do they mean it's terrible but are just trying to be nice?

See what I mean? All of this mental stuff can play havoc with you when you next sit down to write. There is only one sure way to prevent all this and that is to keep your writing to yourself until it's finished!

I'll give you another reason.

Imagine showing someone, a friend say, something you've just written. You know it's not perfect but there are a couple of good lines.

Even if you tell your friend over and over that it's rough and not finished, he or she will still regard it as an example of your work. And if it's bad, that person will always think of your work in those terms – full of mistakes. That's the way people are. They can't help it.

And while we're on the subject, don't ever fall into the trap of giving important people a first draft, especially not a publisher or agent. For the reasons stated in the previous paragraph, it could blow your entire career. I've seen it happen.

Okay, you probably think I'm being paranoid but this is not some dry textbook full of the standard wisdom. This is me talking to you, giving you the best advice I can.

Just so you're convinced, here's another curious phenomenon:

For some inexplicable reason, your spouses will always think they could have written your work better than you!

Never mind that they don't write, don't want to write, or have never given writing a thought, your loved ones think that writing is hard to get right – and that only the very, very best should do it for a living! (Which won't be you, of course.)

However unfairly, your family will judge you against a professionals' finished product.

No matter that the professional has had his manuscript edited and re-edited, that he himself re-wrote it twenty times, that copy-editors, proof readers and editors have been over it with a fine tooth comb – to your family, you are in direct competition with that professional. And if it doesn't shape up, you'd better beware!

You see, readers believe what they see on the page. Writers see words. Readers don't, they see stories, images, emotions. It is the job of the writer to place ideas into the mind of the reader. That is the measure of success, no matter what words are used.

The trouble is, your family has to first overcome the fact that they know you. So you're already at a disadvantage. Next, they will assume that you are in the writing. They will take umbrage if your writing reflects a view they know you don't have, and they will mentally question it. Even if they get as far as believing your writing, they will still be on the lookout for any gaffes that break their concentration. You really have to be doubly good to impress your own family!

Especially when you're starting out.

You see, most readers erroneously believe that all 'good' writers get it right the first time. That all they need to do is sit at the typewriter and pure genius pours forth from their fingertips.

Professional writers will tell you this is pure fantasy.

It is the job of the writer, editor and proof-reader to make the final draft look like it was written effortlessly in one go!

In the same way, modern pop singers record their songs one line at a time, making sure each line is perfect – to give the illusion it was sung in one take.

Also, I would advise that you don't talk about the business of writing to non-writers.

Don't tell people how long it takes you to write things or how easy this and that was.

For a start, it's boring.

How many words you write an hour is completely meaningless to a non-writer. Your family and friends will likely regard you as pretentious if you talk about these things.

You can't explain the business of writing to someone who doesn't do it. Besides, nobody but writers are interested in the first place! So, don't waste you breath.

As I keep on saying: Keep it to yourself!

Mindset

Despite everything you've read from me so far, I think finding the time to write has got less to do with time management than it is about gaining the right mindset. Once you have that, you will find the time.

Getting the right mindset may take years. It may take only as long as it takes to read this book. It's about making a commitment to yourself. If you decide something is vitally important to you, life has a way of organizing itself to help you.

As I've suggested before, in order to achieve this mindset, you may want to use meditation, visualization, whatever.

For you to write a novel quickly and easily, the goal is to create another you – a persona that becomes obsessed with the idea of writing it. And the easiest way to do that is simply to write – whenever you can - and when you're not, at the very least, to think about your writing and planning when you're next going to do it.

And hopefully within the next twenty four hours!

CHAPTER SIX

Why Writers Fail - So You Don't Have To

You'll have noticed that this book is as much about self-motivation as it is about writing. This is because I believe the two are intimately related.

If they weren't, everybody would be writing novels.

It takes a special kind of person to sit and write for no apparent reward. Motivation isn't something you can pull out of the fridge and drink – unfortunately.

Many writers complain about lack of motivation when it comes to their writing - they're too tired, or they're not inspired enough today – all kinds of excuses. Of course, it doesn't matter. Nobody really cares whether you write your novel or not. As I intimated in the previous chapter, some of the people close to you may be secretly pleased that you're having trouble motivating yourself.

You have to work at getting the motivation to write a book. Some writers have it naturally. Others have to push themselves, psyche themselves up as it were. The easiest way to write a novel is - to borrow a phrase from Anthony Robbins – for it to become a "magnificent obsession" for the time you will spend writing it.

I hope your novel will become that by the end of this book.

Why Writing Fails

As I've said, good writing usually comes from a secure, well-motivated and happy writer.

Similarly, bad writing most often comes from an insecure, unmotivated, and unhappy writer. Or else one that is just too lazy to learn some of the basic rules of writing. I've known quite a few.

Incompetence and pigheadedness aside, I believe most bad writing is rooted in fear.

Fear of:

* *Action*
* *Failure*
* *Success*

Fear of Action

Many writers are nervous of taking action. They're afraid that making a commitment to a project will mean hard work. It will also mean that they must finish something – otherwise they will feel as though they have failed. Many writers get stuck in this kind of loop.

They can't start projects because they know deep down they can't finish them. When they do start, they're so convinced they can't finish that the prophecy fulfils itself, thereby further undermining their confidence.

I've known writers who have started half a dozen novels and never finished one. This is tragic – and surprisingly common.

The answer is to start small. Don't go into writing a novel before you've learned how it feels to finish things. Write a couple of short stories. Very short, if need be. Try an article, or a review. Even if it's just a paragraph. Set yourself a target and don't stop until it's over. Done.

This will send a powerful message to your subconscious. And as we have discovered, the subconscious needs these signals badly. It needs to be convinced you have what it takes before you start.

Fear of Failure

All writers fear failure. Some are so afraid that their writing will be bad that they can't start. They ask themselves, What's the point? They tell themselves, I know what I write will be awful. Nobody will like it. Who am I kidding?

As we've learned, these are terrible things to say to your subconscious. They completely undermine your potential success. They may even stop you from writing at all. I've seen it happen – too often.

Remember this: In the long run, it is far better to be blindly optimistic about your work and your capabilities than it is to be "realistic".

How else will you know how good your work can be unless you start and finish it!

Fear of Success

This seemingly bizarre phenomenon is probably not as well understood as it should be.

Why would anyone be afraid of success?

The reasons could be many and complex. This book is probably not the best place to go over all of them. Suffice it to say, there are issues of self-worth at work here. Issues that in all probability date back to childhood.

Parents do not always mean to undermine their children's confidence or damage their self-esteem, but it seems to happen nonetheless. Talk of "not expecting too much from life" and a casual or indifferent attitude towards a child's creativity can cause huge problems later on in life.

I've known many creative people who are stultified by the notion that they don't deserve success – or are not the right type of person to handle it. It takes great strength indeed to counteract these feelings of "never being good enough."

I believe it's the duty of parents to encourage their children's creativity, no matter how bad their initial efforts. Studies have consistently shown that children do much better when they are complimented and made to feel special.

If you are plagued by feelings of inadequacy, I would suggest you read a few of the books I've listed at the back. I would especially recommend Susan Jeffers' book, *Feel the Fear and Do It Anyway*, which has a whole section on this issue of dealing with insecurities that stem from 'bad' parenting.

Writing Demons

There are other reasons why writers fail to achieve their goals. Things you should be aware of so that they don't come back to haunt you in the future.

If you are finding it hard to write then you need to ask yourself the following hard question.

Do I really want to do this?

The answer (if you've read this far!) is probably yes.

If you've ever had trouble writing easily, it might be for the following reasons:

You've outgrown the worldview initially required for your premise

You're trying too hard to be perfect

You're afraid of success, failure or indifference

You've received an emotional shock that has sent you reeling

You're depressed and can't see the point

All of these conditions are transient.

By following the techniques laid in Chapter One, you can effectively reprogram your mind around these problems.

Talk to yourself in positive terms. Imagine a solution, or simply believe that there is one and it will come.

Your goal is clarity of mind.

Preparation

As I've said before, the key to creativity is a relaxed mental state. This is because, under the techniques outlined in this book, you'll be using your subconscious to write your novel. And the subconscious is much easier to access if you are relaxed and clear.

If you try to use your conscious logical side of your mind to write, you'll take forever, as in the traditional image of writers, agonizing over every word. You may have been doing this for years already and might find it a difficult habit to break.

If so, you must learn to change.

Writing with your logical mind not only wastes your time – it's not particularly productive -it can actually harm your creativity. What the ego needs is results – quickly. And that's what letting the subconscious do the writing will provide.

Whilst you are writing you need to switch off your conscious mind. The way to do this is to write fast. Don't edit, don't go back, and don't think about anything but the next line. Let your fingers write or type automatically.

The best piece of advice I've seen regarding this is in Joe Vitale's *Hypnotic Writing*. He suggests, if you write on a computer, that you switch off the screen.

Try it. At first it may seem disorientating but stick with it. It's exactly the right way to increase your output a thousand-fold.

Whereas you might have written two hundred words an hour before, this one technique can increase your output by around ten times! And this is the kind of output you will need to write a novel quickly. If you want to write a novel in a month for instance, you will need to write roughly 2000 to 5000 words a day – and all in an hour or two - or three!

The thing that will surprise you the most is that, contrary to what you might expect, your writing won't be all that bad. Why? Because your subconscious is in control. It won't let you write badly. Its knowledge, talent and genius are superior to your logical, rational self. If anything, you might discover that you have a style different from the one you were used to. I promise you it will be good, more fluid, more in tune with the way the mind works – and one hell of a lot easier to read.

The trick is to write your entire novel this way. You don't have to keep your screen off all the time but train yourself not to go back and look at anything while you're writing.

Just write the whole thing first.

Does this idea excite you? It should. It's an enormously liberating experience.

Of course, there are a few rules to good storytelling that you will need before you start writing. These I have outlined thoroughly in Part Two. I just wanted to give you a taste of what is to come.

As a quick exercise, just to prove what I'm saying, try this.

Think of a scenario – a brief one.

You're in a hospital and you've just woken up. A policeman is standing over you and he wants a statement. He wants to know how you got there.

Don't think too hard. Come up with five trigger words and write them down the left hand side of a piece of paper. For instance:

* *Accident*
* *Car*
* *Girlfriend*
* *Rain*
* *Tree*

Now, take a deep breath and start writing. Don't stop for ten minutes. Use the first word on your list somewhere in your first sentence. Then keep going. Trust that your subconscious will keep you writing – it will.

The trick is not to stop. Don't even give yourself time to think. Just keep your fingers tapping at the keys or the pen sliding along the paper. Whatever you do, don't stop.

Don't correct spelling mistakes or grammatical errors. Just keep going. If you feel that the ideas might not come, incorporate the next word on your list into your next sentence.

At the end of ten minutes, stop.

You should have written anywhere between 200 to 500 hundred words. Do a quick scan. It's not bad is it? Nothing a little tweaking won't fix!

Do the math. 200 words in ten minutes is 1200 words an hour. 500 words in ten minutes is a staggering 3000 words an hour. If you can write like this for two hours a day, you'll easily be able to write an entire first draft of a novel in thirty days – or even less.

Say you take two days to 'prepare' at the beginning of the month, and three days at the end to edit, that still leaves you with 25 days to write roughly 3000 to 4000 words a day.

Go for it. It can be done.

The Power of Belief

One of the exercises you should be doing at this stage is goal visualization.

This is a common enough technique nowadays whereby you imagine the end product of your labors.

To anyone unfamiliar with this procedure, this may sound premature. However, in a practice akin to what sportsmen do – visualizing your success - you should visualize your book as complete, brilliant and faultless.

Imagine how you will feel when you hold the book in your hands and flip through its pages. Imagine the sense of pride you will feel, the sense of achievement.

These feelings are all useful triggers that set the subconscious mind on fire. When your mind believes that the impossible is possible, then you will start to believe it too.

This is a proven technology. Do it.

Imagine yourself going through the whole process of creating a novel. See yourself from the outside, calmly thinking about the book, typing, making notes, getting inspired, motivated, driven.

Enjoy the sense of joy and purpose and love you feel for your writing as you partake in your favorite pastime. This is important. Especially if you're one of those writers prone to blocks. The best way to deal with blocks is prevent them at source – by doing these kinds of exercises – before you start.

This simple process works because it fools the subconscious mind into believing something different from all the negative attitudes you may have built up over the years.

Conclusion

So now you have the clarity, the mindset and the motivation, we're ready to get going...

Hold on to your hat!

Interlude

Congratulations! You made it to Part Two.

Now, if you've just flicked through the beginning part of the book to get to this point, I forbid you to read any further! You want to know why?

The information in this part will not help you if you haven't thoroughly read Part One.

Of course, there are tips and techniques contained from here on in that will make your writing a whole lot easier, give it depth and credibility, and generally help you on the way to creating a novel. But believe me, without having read Part One, this information will be lost on you!

So go back – and start from the beginning!

The point of Part Two is to familiarize you with some of the basic rules of fiction writing. Then Part Three provides an easy to follow 30-day plan to getting that novel down on paper. It's a system developed by talking with all kinds of writers – fiction and non-fiction, good and bad, amateur and professional.

It's simple – deceptively so – but it's effective.

It's hard not to get bogged down with the immensity of writing a novel. Especially if you've never done it before. That's why this book exists. To help you understand the mechanics of getting a book from inside your head and out, on to the page.

After some of the lessons and exercises that follow, your writing should become more real to you than your everyday life. This is good. This is necessary. It is the way of the professional.

Because only when your imaginary world becomes more important to you than your real life, will you know that you just have to start writing.

Follow the lessons carefully. Do not skip them or give them anything less than your full attention. You must do this for the sake of your novel. By the time you start to write, you should see yourself as merely the scribe of actual events.

PART TWO

How to Write Commercial Fiction

Module One

Getting Ideas

The question most asked of an author is undoubtedly, "Where do you get your ideas from?" Most authors I know inwardly groan when they hear it. Why? Because to a working author, ideas are plentiful. The problem is not in finding ideas, it's finding the time to develop them all!

The best way to come up with ideas is to write a lot, regularly and often – at least ten minutes a day. My partner and I write every day – usually all day from around ten till six. Friends have to lever us out of the house at weekends, or we'd write then too.

To us, ideas come flooding. There's something about the process of juggling words that encourages the mind to sift through concepts and ideas automatically. Ask either of us how we generate ideas and we'll both respond by saying we start writing and ideas just seem to appear. Actually too many. I'd probably need several lifetimes to write as much as I'd like to. The hard part is deciding which ideas are worthwhile and can justify the time needed to spend on them.

But if you write infrequently, you might get stuck thinking of things to write about.

So, where do you start looking for ideas?

Most writers employ the 'what if?' scenario. As in, what if grandma was an alien? Or, what if Jack murdered his wife? Or, what if Sarah inherited a million dollars? The answers to the 'what if' questions should lead you to ideas for stories.

Try using the 'what if' question on a daily basis – in the context of your own life at first.

Ask yourself questions regarding all the mundane things you do like eating breakfast and cleaning your teeth. Questions like, what if I found out someone had poisoned my milk? What would happen if my toothbrush turned into a frog? Get used to turning things on their head. Not all of these questions and answers will lead to story ideas but some of them will.

Develop a questioning mind. Take everyday news stories and try fictionalizing them. For example, a politician was recently convicted of hit and run incident. It would be easy to imagine a story in which this incident could illustrate a character trait of an antagonist for instance. Or you could use the incident as the starting point of a short story.

Look at the people around you and in your own mind, imagine them as fictional characters with different names. Look at their motivations and imagine where their opinions and actions might lead them. For example, your mother may have an obsession about your safety. Try imagining her as a character in a story. What might her obsession lead to? What if the mother's daughter did exactly the things the mother feared? You might use the daughter's flight over Mt Everest in a hot-air balloon or her decision to take up scuba diving as the starting point of a story.

If you're stuck for ideas, read more. Reading can easily suggest ideas to you. Read as much as you can in lots of different arenas: fiction, non-fiction, newspapers, magazines, websites, cornflakes packets, anything. Sometimes just a word or two can trigger your mind into working through possible scenarios. This is not plagiarism. It's healthy exercise for your mind.

For example, recently I read an article about dementia. In it there was a passage about a woman who had ceased to recognize her own reflection in the mirror – she thought there was a woman on the other side of a window who kept looking at her. This immediately got me thinking: "How can develop this idea into a story?" After mulling the idea over for a couple of days I decided I could write a story about a little girl whose grandmother was going so senile she thought that a mirror was a window on to another world filled with strangers, and that the story would be about how the little girl helped her grandmother cope with what, for her, was a terrifying ordeal.

Next I came up with a working title, *Nana and the Mirror People*. To me, giving a story idea a title helps give it solidity in my mind. Plus, I can then add the title to my ever increasing 'to do' list!

Once a day write down your ideas, in note form if you don't have much time. Later, expand on the ideas so that you don't forget them. You'll find the more you write, the more ideas will come to you. And, if that doesn't work for you, go back to the 'what if' questions until they do.

You might also like to keep a notebook next to your bed to record your dreams, or at least snatches of them. I find that recording dreams is rarely a successful exercise. But what is useful is that the words on the page can act as a prompt for other, more usable, ideas.

Context

Now, all the ideas in the world won't particularly help you unless you can see them in context.

As soon as you have an idea, your writer's brain should kick in and decide what the idea might lead to. A scene? A short story or a novel? It will be for you to decide.

For example, using the idea of the lady with dementia from above, I decided that the story should be told as a children's picture book. Though I knew I wouldn't be doing the artwork myself, I do know that children's picture books are generally less than 700 words long – sometimes as short as 200. So, seeing the story in the context of a children's picture book enables me to start seeing words and images that will help tell the story.

Try looking at your ideas individually and expand on them until you can see a format in which the idea can be used. For instance, you may have an idea for a murder mystery where a man is trying to find out the identity of a murderer that turns out to be his own wife. You then decide if this will need to be a short story or a novel.

Next, try thinking through a plot. Okay, that may seem hard – a leap. So, what do you do?

Simple, write a few notes about the character of the man – his job, his habits, his motivations. Name him. Then expand these notes further into ideas about where the man might live, which city, what his apartment looks like. Then draw up a tentative plot, like this:

Dennis, 35 year old stockbroker, returns home to find his daughter dead and his wife missing. A ransom note demands one million dollars. He is sick with fear and engages the help of an old school friend to track down the killer.

Get used to developing ideas into synopses. Make it a habit. Not all of your ideas and possible story lines will be inspired. That doesn't matter. What matters is that you're developing the writer's mindset – which sees stories everywhere.

There's a maxim used in the world of TV script writing. It is, "Your first idea is rarely inspired." This truism is used to make sure a writer is never forced to use clichés. The principle is simple. Take your first idea and try to make it better. Then, try again. It's usually the third of fourth idea that will come across as, at least new, if not truly clever.

For instance, you have scene in your story where you introduce a drug dealer. Your first idea would be to no doubt create some sleaze with a bad attitude and little or no communication skills. Think again. It's been done to death. What if (that phrase again!) you broke with the convention and made the drug dealer a nice respectable middle class kid with a degree in engineering? Think again. What if the drug dealer was a female? What if she only deals drugs to pay for her son's education?

Whenever you're inventing fiction, think outside the square. Then, think further out. Your writing will benefit enormously.

The notion that ideas are plentiful should also extend to your possible stories – you should have heaps of them at the end of each week. Plus, you should begin to regard your story ideas as potential 'projects' you might work on in the future.

But here is the important thing: you should be able to evaluate the potential commerciality of these 'projects' before you start writing them. This is an important lesson to learn early on in your writing career because it will become increasingly important as time goes by.

Each time you have created a concrete story idea from your notes, ask yourself, "Who will want to read this? Which publisher might be interested in this?" "Is there a readership out there that wants this type of story?"

This might seem like a premature, even scary thing to do but it is firmly rooted in a working writer's reality. After all, when you finish a novel or a short story, these are the questions you will be asking yourself anyway – and perhaps way too late when you've spent perhaps up to one or two years working on a project you can't find a publisher for.

So, get used to asking these questions now, up front, before you start writing. You'll have success a lot sooner if you do.

EXERCISE

Come up with 10 'what if' scenarios.

Take a week if you have to but make a conscious decision to look at the world around you with new eyes – ones that question what they see. Turn your ideas into short sentences that denote whether each is a scene, a concept, a possible story, or a full blown potential project.

Part 2 of Module One

I don't know about you but I still – after all this time – go into panic mode when I'm about to embark on a new fiction project. And to this day, I'm not sure why.

It's not as if I haven't been doing it for long enough!

I started writing fiction when I was about six, describing trips to the moon, alien encounters (which I wrote as true stories, much to chagrin of my teachers), and mysteries. I wrote my first stage-play when I was nine and a bunch of us put it on in a neighbor's back garden (we charged sixpence for people to get in.) It was a Western I seem to remember, complete with slapstick and fight sequences.

During my adolescent years I wrote many short stories and novels that I never finished – except one called, *Long Enough to Know* which now seems incomprehensible to me – it's all teen angst and has long passages about how sex wasn't for me. Ah, the innocence of youth.

Later, in my twenties, I wrote a lot of plays and scripts for TV and film, some of which actually got performed and made. But that wasn't my focus at the time. I was a full time musician then and I spent much of my time in recording studios and noisy nightclubs when I wasn't lazing on the deck of my houseboat in Chelsea.

Much later, after the time I call the Dark Age (when I worked for six years as a buyer in an investment company in the City of London) I went back to writing, the artist in me re-emerging into the light of creativity like a blinking worm from its self imposed cocoon.

Nowadays I write fiction mainly for pleasure, when I have spare time, which is not often enough for me. Most of my time is spent teaching writing through courses and books - which I enjoy immensely.

Fear

Sometimes, when we think too much about writing, we create barriers to action in our minds. Worrying about our next project can get so bad that we become afraid of taking action. We may even begin to fear the project. We fear failure, or an inability to live up to our own expectations.

It can become a Catch-22 situation. The more we fear starting a project, the more difficult the project becomes in our mind.

This is self defeating. You have to stop thinking about your project and just get on and begin it. The only way to get over writing problems is to write. No amount of thinking or worrying or analysis will cut it. You must begin.

You must write and not fear what will end up on the page. It doesn't matter whether your writing is any good at this stage. It doesn't matter that what you've written might be bad. The only thing that matters at this stage is to get used to writing – and often.

Procrastination

In a world full of duties and distractions it's too easy to put things off – especially writing, which others especially might regard as a frivolous use of your time. It's not.

To deal with delay you need to set goals. Even just tiny ones.

You see, the reason why we put off jobs is that we get overwhelmed by the prospect of doing something we think will require vast amounts of time. But this is a mental issue that doesn't reflect reality. The reality is that if we give something time, then the 'doing' will take care of itself. The trick is not to fear the project as a whole and keep breaking it down into little, doable, chunks.

Whenever you fear a writing project, mentally cut it in half.

If the prospect of doing half still seems too daunting, cut it in half again. Keep breaking down the task until you get something you can do in five or ten minutes for example.

Too many writers set a goal like: "Plot the book" and never get around to it because plotting a book may take several hours, so they put it off.

What you need to do is put aside 10 minutes per day to work on the plot and/or tell yourself you'll at least begin to work on the plot. Then set a realistic deadline for completing the plot. Don't be too hard on yourself at first though, take baby steps if you have to.

Anxiety

You may put things off to the extent that you begin to get anxious just thinking about your next writing project or book. There is only one way to deal with this and that is to begin. And beginning means writing. Words on the page – no matter how rough they may be.

Whenever I'm feeling anxious over some writing, if not sure where I'm going to begin etc, I make notes – headings mainly that will act as a prompt to me in the future. So, for instance, as I began thinking about my last novel, I made the following notes:

Prologue: murder

Chapter 1, introduce Patrick

Chapter 2, Judith called to crime scene

Chapter 3, Patrick is arrested.

And so on. To me, the act of making notes (headings) diffuses the tension of inactivity. It also helps me to get some idea of where to take the plot.

I find another neat trick is to make notes on the ending too. That way, I don't feel I am writing with no end in sight, wondering where to go next.

Lack of Inspiration

Sometimes we get stuck wondering what to write about. This is common. But wondering isn't writing. Writing is writing. Putting words on paper has a way of firing up the brain and provoking inspiration, even if you have to force it sometimes.

My partner, a full time fiction writer says that whenever she doesn't feel inspired, she fakes it, telling her mind that she is inspired – and guess what? Her mind complies.

Here's another trick that I use.

If you having trouble coming up with things to write about, don't sit and think about it. That won't help. You need to address the problem by writing. Try talking to the page, actually tell it you can't think of anything to say. Ask your mind for inspiration by writing down that request.

For instance, you might write, "What shall I write about today? Hmm, I'm not sure. Come on brain, give me something to write about."

You'll find this exercise is a great way of kick-starting your creativity. Time spent staring into space is wasted time. The only time that is useful to you as a writer is when you're writing.

Self Doubt

Self doubt about your abilities is another killer. I wrote an entire section on this in the previous section. You probably remember.

But again, self doubt is a mental issue that happens when you're not writing. Just know that self doubt is normal – all writers are plagued by it at least sometimes.

You just have to make sure it doesn't stifle your creativity. And the only way to do that is to write more. Just do it, as Nike say. Worry later if you want to – but just get something, anything, down first.

Notebooks can be useful for jotting down ideas but to me their main function to get you used to writing. They also teach you to translate the world around you into words, which is the most important thing. Use them often - especially if you have problems motivating yourself to write. Later, when you're writing regularly, you probably won't need them.

Before that time, whenever you stop for a cup of tea or coffee, open your notebook - or tablet - and write something there. Anything. It doesn't have to be profound or even special. Just say hello to your notebook and write about anything – the weather, what you're worrying about, what you're going to watch on TV tonight – and sure, write down what you think of things, of people, of places. It's all useful to you because it's making you think - and act - like a writer. It's teaching your brain that this is what you do – you write things down.

Journals and diaries serve much the same purpose. I don't know about you but I find reading my old diaries rather tedious. I keep thinking I'm going to come across something profound, witty, or important but it's rarely there. But what is there is evidence that I write, that I'm a writer.

Some people like to use writing prompts – little brain teasers that set them off. I rarely use them because I don't need a prompt to get me going. A blank screen will do that for me.

I think the trick is not to think too hard about writing. Just to do it.

Get used to writing 50 or 100 word passages on any given topic.

For instance, make a heading like "50 words on trees" then write down your thoughts. They don't have to clever or insightful. You can just as easily write: Trees are green and brown. They have leaves on them and I fell out of one when I was a kid. It doesn't matter what you write, just that you are writing.

You'll find that these short passages will help galvanize you towards writing longer and longer passages. Over time, these short passages will help you think more confidently about writing short stories or chapters of your novel.

What you must not do is worry about the quality of your writing. Don't edit or correct things. Just get used to writing words down.

And if you're really stuck, try copying something out of a book. Do anything that tells your brain that you put words on pages. That you are a writer.

Time Management

Finding time to write can be a challenge, especially if you have children, work nine to five, or have a busy social life.

The simple fact is you have to find the time.

Whether that be in front of the TV or late at night, early in the morning, during work breaks, rest breaks or when you're traveling, you have to become obsessed with the idea of making time – for yourself and for your writing.

For about a week, at the end of each day, make a note of how you spent your time. Are there any gaps there you could utilize? Are there errands you could have combined that would have freed up more time?

Look at the time you spend watching TV. Calculate the hours per week. I bet you'll be surprised. Even the most ardent anti TV people watch around five or six hours of TV a week. Most of us watch a lot more. Can you imagine how much you can write in five or six hours?

There's no point wishing your life away thinking, "One day I'll take off a couple of days, weeks, or months and then write." Trust me, it'll never happen. You have to make writing time now, build it into your day, even if the moments are stolen – a few minutes here, a few there.

Writing for long periods is what professionals do, yes, but they all had to start somewhere. Stephen King spent years writing after work before he sold his first novel. Most budding fiction writers have to do that too nowadays because nobody, not unless you're Dan Brown or JK Rowling, gets paid upfront for writing fiction.

Besides, we all write for the love of it first – and for the money later. Don't we?

Develop your love of writing now, and from now on give yourself a million reasons to write. Then, just do it. I promise you the time will, almost miraculously, begin to appear. Ask any committed writer. This is how it works.

Module Two

Living the Dream

So far we've looked at getting the motivation to write and finding the time amidst our busy schedules. In this lesson we will be involved in something more 'spiritual' as we get to grips with the writing process. We'll be looking at what it actually means to be a writer, and more importantly, what it means to be a successful, popular and commercial writer.

I'm assuming you're reading this book because you want to be published by mainstream publishers - or to sell books to a host of readers and fans. I hope that's the case. If it is, then I want you to absorb the following notion:

If you want to make a living as a popular novelist, then you need to write popular novels.

If necessary, read the above sentence again and really think about what it means.

Basically it means that if you want to be a successful writer, your surest route is to write for the market. This might also mean that the kind of stories you want to write are not necessarily those that a reader wants to read.

This is an important distinction because it's imperative you understand, right from the outset, if you're writing popular fiction, you are not writing primarily for yourself.

Okay, you must enjoy what you do, that's for sure, but remember, you are writing for your readers first and yourself second. Take this one idea onboard, absorb it into your psyche, and you'll be published, maybe even famous, before you know it!

What it Means to be a Writer

Every great calling comes with great responsibility. From this moment on you have a duty: to align who you are as a person with how you come across as a writer.

This means you must be honest, have integrity and be able to write convincing fiction without irony, cynicism, self-consciousness or affectation. This is not as hard as it sounds.

For many new writers, being honest can seem daunting, perhaps even terrifying. To bare your soul on the page leaves you vulnerable to attack, which is why criticism can hurt so much. You feel as though people are not criticizing your writing, but criticizing you, attacking you right where it hurts. But remember this. The more honest you are, the more you bare of yourself, the more appealing and effective your writing becomes.

Conversely, the more you hide your real self, the more you hide behind words or use them to deflect readers from getting to know you, the more disservice you do to your writing. Readers are not easily fooled. They might not know why they dislike a writer, but they have a sixth sense for dishonesty, for being patronized or misled.

Think of the great fiction writers you know. Do you have any doubt that these authors believe in their characters? That they aren't describing people and places and actions that seem entirely real to them? Of course not. This is what marks out a great writer. Not brilliant technique or the use of clever metaphors — but simple honesty.

To become a great fiction writer you need to have a strong vision in mind and do your level best to transfer that vision on to the page.

Mindset

John Braine (author of *Room at the Top*) once said, "A writer is someone who counts words." At first, this sounds flippant and simplistic. But the longer you write – as in the years you put in as a writer – the more true this maxim becomes.

Because writing for a living, and more especially writing fiction for a living, is about discipline. It's about knowing you only have a certain number of words to get across a scene, an emotion, a chapter, a theme, a whole novel, you name it, there's only so much time and wordage you can use to get across your idea, your meaning, your point.

Look at submission guidelines for novels, non-fiction, short stories, articles, newspaper columns. Get past the guidelines and it's all about word count. Hence, whenever you are asked to write something or you feel an urge to write about a subject or theme, your automatic first response should be: "How many words do I have?" Because this affects everything that follows.

But writing is not so much about how many words you can write on something, it's about knowing when to stop, and move on.

Professional writers spend much of their time deciding how best to use time, what to focus on, what to write next – so that their efforts are concentrated on what really matters to them, their readers (including editors, agents, publishers etc) – and their writing.

Spend a little time now deciding what's important about your next writing project.

If it's a novel, think about how long it will take to tell the story. Not just in terms of time but in terms of effort too - how long will you spend on your characters as opposed to the action? How much effort, compared to other writing activities, will it require to set your scenes, to create locations, to develop your plots, to tell the story? Time is finite and you need to get a balance now between what is practical and what is unrealistic.

Letting your mind run over these issues is all good preparation for the writing to come. But remember, it's not a substitute. As I stressed in the last module, you only make progress when you are writing. All else is air, insubstantial space – and wasted writing time.

Fiction Matters

My Dad, like many people, says he doesn't like to read fiction because it's not true – so what's the point? This is a man, like many of his generation, that delights in endless documentaries and books about the Second World War but who will pout when forced to endure a romantic comedy or even an episode of *Law and Order*.

On the rare occasion I've managed to tie him to a chair and show him one of my stories, he will pretend to read for a while before handing me back the book saying, "Just tell me what happens at the end." To which, as is often the case with fiction, there's not always an easy answer!

What Dad's missing, of course, is that fiction is often more true than fact.

Fiction lets writers and readers explore the profound truths of life and our experience of it. Fiction is the means by which writers show there's meaning and purpose beyond mere existence and that, if nothing else, we're supposed to enjoy ourselves while we're here!

On a quantum level, the building blocks of life are chaotic and seemingly random. And yet out of this chaos, life is not only created but, according to the latest theories, mathematically inevitable. Our appearance on Earth may have taken 200 million years but we arrived eventually and have since seen it as our duty to describe our experience of 'being alive' and what that might mean.

This quest for truth, whether it be by merely describing the experience or by trying to order it into meaningful chunks, seems innate in us. As though by the act of creation we are emulating and giving thanks to mother nature. By writing we become mini gods who create worlds within worlds, life within life, order from chaos.

This profound responsibility should therefore not be taken lightly. Our job as fiction writers is to entertain and inform, yes, but it is also to enlighten and bring hope.

Trust and the Author/Reader Pact

By reading your fiction, the reader has given over a part of themselves to you. They are trusting you, for the duration of their time reading, not to insult, annoy or mentally abuse them. In return you must treat your reader with the utmost respect.

This means giving your all, fulfilling your commitment to entertain and enlighten them.

In nebulous terms this means making your story the best that it can be – or at least the best you can make it.

In practical terms it means attention to detail: punctuation, grammar and spelling are all just as important as the story. Ask any editor and they will confirm this is the case. Think of it this way: any sloppiness on your part, no matter how trivial it may seem to you, is a slap in the face to your reader. Be meticulous when you present your work – and hold it back until it's as perfect as you can make it.

More on this later in the course. I just wanted you to be aware, even at this early stage, that presentation is extremely important, especially to your very first readers: usually agents and publishers. They too, are trusting you to deliver the goods and deserve your hard work, humility and respect.

It's even more important of course if you're self publishing, that your book looks as professional as possible. There's nothing worse than gaining the trust of a reader - and having them hand over money for your self-published book - only to abuse that trust by presenting them with bad formatting, atrocious punctuation and questionable grammar - a scenario which happens all too often these days!

The Rules of Engagement

In later modules we'll be getting down to the nitty gritty on how to write great, saleable fiction. We'll be looking at everything from sentence construction to characterization and plotting, from improving your personal writing style to building brilliant stories. But for now, I want to leave you with something to think about.

Publishers often say they're looking for that little something extra in a manuscript that sets it apart from all the others. As a consequence I'm often asked, "What is it? What is this "little something extra" and where can I find it?"

Well, let me tell you. There's no need to go hunting around in books and tutorials to find it. There's no need to study all the classics – old and modern - trying to quantify it. Why? Because you already possess it.

(Drum roll, please) It's you.

That little something extra is the unique you that no-one else can begin to emulate. Only you can see the world the way you do and only you can describe it in your own way. Therefore, as you write, remember to put as much of yourself into your work as you can. Don't hold back, don't be afraid to bare your soul and let the reader inside your head and your heart.

They'll love you for it.

And publishers will see it too: that "little something extra" is you!

EXERCISE

Write a couple hundred words on who you are, what kind of stories you want to write and why. Also commit to noting down how you intend to find the time and motivation to write.

Be as detailed, honest, and specific as you like.

Module Three

Characterization

Up until now we've looked at motivation, creating realistic writing goals for yourself and acquiring the professional writer's mindset. Now, we're going to look at the first of the more practical writing matters.

Characters

First of all, for the record, I should state my position on storytelling. If you're familiar with my approach to fiction, it should be obvious to you by now but here goes:

There is no story without characters, therefore, do not try to plot a story until you have its characters firmly in mind.

Novice writers are often asked to complete complex exercises relating to character creation that they may never use once they are professional.

As always in my courses, it is not my intention to teach you anything but the easiest and most practical writing methods, so I won't be expecting you to complete long and pointless character analyses. We'll keep it simple – at least for now!

Creating Characters

There are a lot of silly exercises and strategies available out there that do little to bring a character into sharp focus. I don't hold with the idea of creating these ten to twenty page questionnaires where you have to list everything about a character including their shoe size, likes and dislikes, blood type and star sign. Mainly because I don't feel this is useful work – it's just putting off what's necessary later on: the writing, where character description and development become more pertinent and relevant to the story.

So what's the best way to go about inventing – and describing – characters?

Think about the people you know and like. How much do you really know about them? How would you describe them? Most of us can sum up what people are like, even those closest and most familiar to us, in a couple of short lines. Why not do the same for your own creations? Why waste valuable writing time on character information you may never use?

Short descriptions – call them prompts – are enough. For instance, *John is tall, fair-haired and handsome in a Harrison Ford kind of way. He's an accountant and likes to jog at the weekend.*

Or, *Maddy is twenty six, a slinky blonde, a bit full of herself if you ask me. She likes to party, talks fast in a loud voice and mostly wears black. I guess she thinks it makes her look sexy.*

When it comes to your own characters, it's not about how much of them you can describe – but what they mean to you that's important. Of course, for the purposes of outlining characters to ourselves it's important that we commit to paper how that person looks, acts and feels – in note form if necessary. It's more than enough to be going along with at this early stage. What's more important is that we can 'see' the characters in our mind's eye and we know them in the same way as we know our family members and friends.

For the purposes of keeping things simple, here's how to outline a character to yourself, without spending hours filling out questionnaires:

1. Name

2. *Age*
3. *Race*
4. *Body type*
5. *Agenda*
6. *Motivation*
7. *Goals*

The last three items become the most important later on, when you're writing. The first four should be enough to enable you to get a good 'fix' on your character, from which you can later build a convincing portrait.

Of course these small sketches don't address the depth of your characters but that's what the writing is for!

One of the problems with creating large character analyses is that once you've written down everything about your character, there's very little you will want to say about them within your writing. Indeed, much of your detail will be irrelevant to your character description and may even hinder your story. Characters should be flexible, organic, able to surprise you – just like real people.

I'm not suggesting this minimalist approach be rigidly adhered to at all times.

During the writing of your novel, it might be a good idea to create card files of your main characters that list their main attributes - to which you can add notes to as you go along. Things like hair color, habits, usual clothing etc become more relevant as you progress through your MS. Sometimes it's useful to have the cards somewhere at hand to refer to, in case you forget little details, just so that you are consistent.

These days I use Scrivener to collect my character snapshots all in one place - because it's close to the manuscript. One day, I'd suggest you do the same. Scrivener is a godsend to novel writers!

Visualization

When you have characters in mind, especially if they're the protagonist and the antagonist, spend some time with your eyes closed trying to visualize them. See them in your mind's eye and consciously regard them with affection. Spend some time admiring them, making them as real to you as you can. Then ask yourself questions.

What do you like about this person? What are their good and bad traits? How will they react when spoken to, provoked, challenged?

Get to grips with how their thought patterns work, how their personal agendas will affect the world around them and the people in it.

Getting a feel for your characters in this way better reflects reality. We all have agendas, whether it is to be loved, respected or merely listened to. This affects the way we interact with the world. It is seen in our outer shell – the person who others see. When we look at our characters as though they're real people, we're more likely to make them believable to our readers.

To create compelling, real characters, we need to take this one step further. Most people live in relative harmony with their environments. The best fictional characters do not. We need to put our real people in situations whereby they can work on their agendas and achieve their goals. We need to put them at odds with the people and or the locations and circumstances they exist within. In this sense it's not always necessary to create characters with great depth. The truth is some strong consistent characters in modern fiction are fairly thinly drawn.

For example, Dan Brown's character, Robert Langdon, is a fairly two dimensional chap without much depth or even many issues. We know he's middle aged, is a professor and has an attraction to unraveling mysteries. He's also claustrophobic and afraid of heights – but who isn't? These traits don't make him much different from most other people. What makes him compelling is that these characteristics are relevant and continually tested by the stories he is involved in. We have a sense he is growing in that he's overcoming obstacles and coming closer to truth – but that's all.

Reader Identification

No amount of detail or exposition will help a reader bond with your characters unless they like them. This doesn't necessarily mean they have to be likeable. But there must be a means by which the reader identifies with the characters.

In *The Outsider*, Albert Camus presents us with a not very likeable lead character. He's shallow and narcissistic in much the same way as the lead character in *American Psycho*. What makes these characters work is not that they are likeable but that they seem engaged in activities – listening to music, reading books, going to work – that we can relate to. And as much as we don't want to consider the implications, we can see ourselves in the character and follow them into the murders they commit.

Harry Potter is perhaps the most famous current example of a character without depth that remains compelling – purely because he is so easy for ten to fifteen year boys to relate to. He's a teenage equivalent of 'everyman' – he has dreams, doesn't believe he's capable of them but finds reserves within himself (magic in most cases) to overcome his obstacles.

Character Empathy

Many great novels of the past appear to explore character. Dostoevsky, Jane Austen, the Brontes, Conrad, Dickens took character analysis to the nth degree. Even today, many romances and even horror novels explore the human condition and how we can overcome our limitations and desires to become more rounded people.

However, James Patterson, Patricia Cornwell, Kathy Reichs, Dan Brown, John Grisham, Stephen King to name but a few of the world's best selling authors show us that character development per se is not necessarily the focus of the modern fiction writer.

The important aspect is story – and how the story affects the characters. Your job as a modern fiction writer is to create characters that readers do not feel intimidated by and with whom they want to spend the duration of a novel. To do this, you must be honest – and use your own personality to give your characters life. Give them those little foibles that make us all unique and personable.

Read modern novels and you'll notice it's the little details that help draw us in to a hero's life. We like to know what they eat, how they organize their lives, what they do at work and how they interact with the people around them. Empathy is created by getting the reader to feel they know the character and how they will respond – and to be cheering them on.

You have much leeway in this regard because, if you write with clarity and logic, the reader is more likely to know how your characters will react, and support their actions, even if they wouldn't react that way themselves.

Character Depth

It's very easy to get hung up on character development to the detriment of story. Many writers say (at the beginning of a project in particular) they want to explore character traits and emotions and forget that the way to do this is to show instead of tell.

Too much focus on the internal emotional landscape of a character can slow a story to a stop. I see it all the time in novice manuscripts. It can be very dull to read.

Rather than explaining how a person is feeling about an event – taking a more passive internalized view of characters – we should be concentrating on how we can show the person is acting and reacting to the story's events.

Character development, growth and change should be the result of the story, not its reason to be. In modern popular fiction character development should be incidental to the plot, rather than the sole reason for the novel's existence.

So, don't get hung up on, "I want the characters to experience grief, courage and whatever." Instead decide now to SHOW how the characters react and what actions they take as a RESULT of experiencing those emotions. Characters who take action and actively seek out solutions to obstacles are far more compelling than those that 'think a lot' and appear to be stifled by their indecision. People don't want to read about characters who can't see a way out of their problems. They want to believe in characters that can move on and find a better result – just as they might wish they could do themselves in their own lives.

Readers want characters that are heroes, people who can save the world. Readers want protagonists who can defeat the bad guys, no matter what the odds. Readers want characters that make sense of their world and their lives.

There's no point reading about a static world where there is no growth and change. As fiction writers we need to present heroes and heroines that are slightly larger than life, that are more capable, who have pro-active attitudes and are always prepared to confront their demons, antagonists, problems and obstacles.

Creating Characters for a Series

The goal of many professional writers is to pen a series. It's ironic then that one of the challenges for the serial writer is not to develop their characters too much.

Sue Grafton's character, Kinsey Millhone, is a prime example. When the series is over there will be twenty-six books, all featuring a middle aged female detective who does progress through her life – different relationships, altering circumstances etc – but essentially remains static. She's the same person in every book.

As is the case with many of the serialized characters to we know and love today. Sherlock Holmes, Rumpole of the Bailey, Kaye Scarpetta, Harry Potter, Dirk Pitt, Miss Marple – they are all essentially static characters that interact with new circumstances but rarely change their personalities, even their situations.

Interesting, Strong, Exciting

Sustained character development is ultimately a personal issue. For the purposes of most novel length fiction however, you will be concerned with characters with goals they either achieve or they don't.

One of the ways to make characters more believable and interesting is to give them individual quirks and mannerisms. All kinds of things will do. A way of walking, flicking their hair, little habits, ways of looking at people. It's important that your people are instantly recognizable and different.

Everything from not having names that are too similar to other characters, to creating traits that are individual. Tall and short. Fat or thin. Personal or family problems, issues, whatever. Minor characters too, often have to be more pronounced to make them recognizable. Oh, and don't be afraid to make minor characters a little 'louder than real life', so the reader doesn't get lost in amongst them all.

EXERCISE

Draw up 200 to 500 word sketches for the main characters of your next projected novel. Don't forget to include their motivations, the reasons for them and their agendas and goals.

Remember, there should rarely be more than five main characters in a modern popular novel. More and you're writing an epic. Keep it simple – at least for time being, okay?

Module Four

Story Creation

This module we get stuck in to the fundamentals of story creation – how it's best achieved with depth and the clarity of vision that is important to how your novel will finally look and feel.

Apologies for the fact this may require some work on your part, even if that means just making lots of notes. It's important at this stage to really steep yourself in the mythos that will become your novel.

Getting to know your story intimately is good though because it will make the story so much easier to write. The aim of this module is to help you create a story that you will be able to visualize in depth – and describe as 'real.'

Plot

As I intimated in the last module, characters first, plot second.

Suffice it to say, based on the experience of 99% of authors I've known, read about and worked with, if you don't do it this way around, you'll get stuck. And if you don't get stuck you'll end up getting a lot of rejections that say things like, "I didn't believe in your characters," or "Your characterization needs work," etc.

So, what's a plot?

Below I have listed what are considered to be the basic plots used since the beginning of time. All stories, it's posited, can be broken down into 3, 7, 20 or 36 basic plots. Having said that, there's really only one that works – every time.

"An individual or group of individuals must overcome a problem or set of obstacles to achieve a satisfactory outcome."

On the simplest level, this might manifest itself in "Character faces monster", whether that monster be a nameless evil, an adulterous spouse, a job loss, or a crisis of conscience. The way a good story is told too, remains consistent. As in:

1. Introduction of Character
2. Explanation of Problem
3. Rising Conflict / Drama / Action
4. Climax
5. Denouement

As long as you have these key elements in your story, you won't go far wrong. I've seen many stories over the years (by unpublished authors mostly) that attempt to circumvent these requirements and produce work that these authors regard as more "original". However, these stories turn out to be generally flat and lifeless – wandering and aimless. Readers have a need to be engaged in a story and rooting for characters to overcome their obstacles is a sure-fire way of ensuring that engagement.

Brainstorming Your Story

Begin by writing down the names of your characters at the top of a sheet of paper. I suggest just three main characters to begin with.

Then, make notes on their personalities and their agendas. By way of example, let me show you what I have for my current novel.

Patrick: An aging rock musician, forced to confront an unknown killer, who seems determined to avenge a death Patrick apparently caused.

Judith: A middle aged black police chief, out to catch the killer, protect Patrick and prove herself as a female cop.

Jimmy: Eventually revealed as the twisted killer after a long and obstacle laden journey.

Do something similar for your own story.

Now it's time to brainstorm ideas.

How will your characters interact?

How will they help and hinder each other?

What situations will they find themselves in?

What obstacles will they face?

How long will it take them to overcome obstacles to their success?

As with any writing exercise, it's best to write down the answers to these questions – in note form at least, to help the ideas solidify in your mind.

The Opening Event

Next, pick an opening event. Your story should ideally begin close to a crisis point, where your lead character and his/her problem or dilemma is introduced. The genre you are writing in will determine the kind of character and their problem. For instance, in a romance, a female might be introduced at the point at which she is crossing swords with a potential partner. In a thriller, your character may be confronted by the result of a killer's handiwork. In a psychological drama, a character may be introduced wrestling with an event or crisis or issues that define the point or theme of the story.

In a more literary novel – as is the fashion - you might want to introduce a story near its eventual conclusion before backtracking to a point where you begin the story proper.

A few years back it was considered customary to open a novel with a few pages of gentle exposition to set the scene before the crisis point was revealed. In more modern novels however, this is no longer the case. Too much exposition up front and your novel's impact will fall flat. It's best now to introduce the crisis point first – or at least an intriguing question – and then fall back on exposition to better explain the context of your crisis / question / character dilemma.

Developing the Story

From your opening event you will then need to explore "Cause and Effect."

The next event or scene in your story should happen as a direct result of the preceding scene. Don't fall into the trap of inventing another event that is outside of or not directly precipitated by your characters. In other words, your character's reaction to the opening event should in most cases "cause" the following scene.

Likewise, each event or scene thereafter should be follow the same rule. This causes this, causes this, causes this, and so on.

By way of example in my own story – again:

The murder at the beginning of the story causes the police woman's involvement which causes her to suspect Patrick, which causes his involvement in the hunt for the killer, which causes the killer to react etc., etc.

You'll find that if you do not adhere to these cause and effect rules, your story can quickly become illogical, thereby losing the attention and more importantly, the trust of the reader.

Keep noting down scenes and events that follow the characters' journey towards the resolution of their goals.

Then, deliberately insert obstacles along the way.

For instance, in a romance you may insert a series of misunderstandings between the protagonists that appear to thwart their union. In a thriller or mystery you might introduce false clues, dead ends and reveal the killer and/or secret is more cunning as the story unfolds. In a more cerebral tale you may have a character that confronts more and more psychological demons or uncooperative friends, lovers and authority figures. In Horror or SF or Fantasy, the protagonist's enemies should become larger, more powerful, more capable, more life-threatening as the story progresses.

The rule is: Don't make it too easy for the main characters to resolve their problems/ dilemmas. But also, the dilemmas / problems / obstacles must seem real and credible - and appropriate to your characters' situations.

The subtlety of your plot will in large part be dependent on your particular scenario, where your story is set, what its backdrop is, how your characters deal with their issues. But don't forget that, as you map out the scenes in your story to their eventual resolution, nothing is set in stone. You can always change things. Many authors will use this process to create a draft plot, then mull it over for a couple of weeks, perhaps months before they commit to using the plot as a template for a novel.

And, as you might expect, some details will change anyway, as you write. Having said that, I do believe you should have a definite ending in mind before you begin the writing proper. I've come to blows with other writers over this point in the past but bitter experience has shown me that writers who fail to map out an ending are almost always those that fail to finish their novels. I have a million theories for this but mulling them over – and describing them in detail - won't get around the need for a practical solution, which is clearly: Know Your Ending!

Card Systems vs. File Systems

When it comes to plotting, there's really only one guideline: Do what works for you.

I find that I deliberately use different techniques for developing different stories. I do this to keep the approach to each new idea fresh. Using the same technique can stultify the creative process at times and I like to keep myself excited with each new project hence, I try to find new ways of developing them each time.

I know some authors swear by them, but I rarely use index cards to organize my plots. I generally list and number my plot points on a Word or Scrivener document and re-arrange them as I see the story grow more logical in my mind. I find this approach works well because I can add notes to the document and expand some of the plot points into scenes and chapters without referring to anything but the main document. Your best way may be different from mine.

At the very least I suggest that you create a file – whether on a computer or a real cardboard file, where you store all the relevant information for each novel in one place.

I've used a few software programs that promise to make this process easier – in fact you'd be forgiven for thinking these software programs can actually write your novel for you! The truth is, however, these software programs are no substitute for actual writing and most of them are really only glorified filing systems, rarely worth the time and money spent on them.

Mind-Mapping

I know, too, that some writers like to use mind-mapping diagrams to help them fathom the intricacies of their plot and their characters' relationships. You can spend hours writing text in bubbles and drawing lines in between them but to what end I'm not sure.

Writing is for the most part a linear process that requires a logical succession of statements and proposals – something that a mind map doesn't portray or illuminate. If you like mind-maps, enjoy creating them but again, they are no real substitute for the actual writing.

Genre Requirements.

If you keep getting stuck with your plotting, take a break and do some reading. Read especially fiction that is closest in genre to that you wish to write in. Sometimes a completely unrelated story – and how it's being told by its author – can help trigger in you the tools necessary for understanding how you yourself want to tell stories.

This is not plagiarism, it is merely a kind of mental fitness regime. For starters, it's very important for the first time published author to show potential publishers that you understand where you sit within a genre. That you have studied the craft and the competition and know your parameters. Too often beginners try to create complicated monolithic first novels that contain everything they have ever thought and dreamt. This is a mistake when all that is really required is that you service the expectations of your reader. Go too far outside of your particular genre requirements and you risk alienating publishers, agents and readers alike.

Thinking Outside the Square

As I believe I've mentioned before, your first idea is rarely your best. First ideas tend to be borne out your major influences and as a consequence can seem derivative, at best and at worst, cliché.

Get used to rejecting your first idea, even the second, and plumping for a more original, more personal take on characterization, story lines and plot twists. This will stand you in good stead throughout your career as a writer. Indeed, it's expected of you.

Sub Plots

I'm not a big fan of deliberately crafting subplots and then grafting them on to a story. Whenever I come across them in fiction, I tend to tune out. I believe the best subplots grow out of the story as you're writing – and may need editing down or deleting towards end of the novel writing process.

Don't worry about seemingly loose story threads as you write your first draft. Sometimes they can lead you in interesting directions. But be aware that the main thrust of your writing should concentrate itself on the primary story, your vision for the novel.

Below are the currently accepted basic plot-lines that form all of fiction, for your information - and inspiration!

The Seven Basic Plots, Christopher Booker

1. Overcoming the monster -- defeating some force which threatens... e.g. most Hollywood movies; *Star Wars, James Bond.*

2. The Quest -- typically a group set off in search of something and (usually) find it. e.g. *Watership Down, Pilgrim's Progress.*

3. Journey and Return -- the hero journeys away from home to somewhere different and finally comes back having experienced something and maybe changed for the better. e.g. *Wizard of Oz, Gulliver's Travels.*

4. Comedy - not necessarily a funny plot. Some kind of misunderstanding or ignorance is created that keeps parties apart which is resolved towards the end bringing them back together. e.g. *Bridget Jones Diary, War and Peace.*

5. Tragedy - Someone is tempted in some way, vanity, greed etc and becomes increasingly desperate or trapped by their actions until at a climax they usually die. Unless it's a Hollywood movie, when they escape to a happy ending. e.g. *Devil's Advocate, Hamlet.*

6. Rebirth - hero is captured or oppressed and seems to be in a state of living death until it seems all is lost when miraculously they are freed. e.g. *Snow White.*

7. Rags to Riches - self explanatory. e.g. *Cinderella* & derivatives (all 27,000 of them)!!!

According to Jessamyn West, an IPL volunteer librarian, the seven basic plots are:

1 - [wo]man vs. nature
2 - [wo]man vs. man
3 - [wo]man vs. the environment
4 - [wo]man vs. machines/technology
5 - [wo]man vs. the supernatural
6 - [wo]man vs. self
7 - [wo]man vs. god/religion

There are also claims made that there are seven basic needs to a story line.

1. A hero – the person through whose eyes we see the story unfold, set against a larger background.

2. The hero's character flaw – a weakness or defense mechanism that hinders the hero in such a way as to render him/her incomplete.

3. Enabling circumstances – the surroundings the hero is in at the beginning of the story, which allow the hero to maintain his/her character flaw.

4. An opponent – someone who opposes the hero in getting or doing what he/she wants. Not always a villain. For example, in a romantic comedy, the opponent could be the man or woman whom

the hero seeks romance with. The opponent is the person who instigates the life-changing event.

5. The hero's ally – the person who spends the most time with the hero and who helps the hero overcome his/her character flaw.

6. The life-changing event – a challenge, threat or opportunity usually instigated by the opponent, which forces the hero to respond in some way that's related to the hero's flaw.

7. Jeopardy – the high stakes that the hero must risk to overcome his/her flaw. These are the dramatic events that lend excitement and challenge to the quest.

Foster-Harris. The Basic Patterns of Plot. Norman: University of Oklahoma Press, 1959. Foster-Harris contends that there are three basic patterns of plot (p. 66):

1. "Type A, happy ending'"; Foster-Harris argues that the "Type A" pattern results when the central character (which he calls the "I-nitial" character) makes a sacrifice (a decision that seems logically "wrong") for the sake of another.

2. "Type B, unhappy ending'"; this pattern follows when the "I-nitial" character does what seems logically "right" and thus fails to make the needed sacrifice.

3. "Type C,' the literary plot, in which, no matter whether we start from the happy or the unhappy fork, proceeding backwards we arrive inevitably at the question, where we stop to wail, "This pattern requires more explanation." (Foster-Harris devotes a chapter to the literary plot.) In short, the "literary plot" is one that does not hinge upon decision, but fate; in it, the critical event takes place at the beginning of the story rather than the end. What follows from that event is inevitable, often tragedy. (This in fact coincides with the classical Greek notion of tragedy, which is that such events are fated and inexorable.)

Polti, Georges. The Thirty-Six Dramatic Situations. trans.
Lucille Ray.

Polti claims to be trying to reconstruct the 36 plots that Goethe
alleges someone named [Carlo] Gozzi came up with. (In the
following list, the words in parentheses are our annotations to try to
explain some of the less helpful titles.):

1. *Supplication (in which the Supplicant must beg something from Power in authority)*
2. *Deliverance*
3. *Crime Pursued by Vengeance*
4. *Vengeance taken for kindred upon kindred*
5. *Pursuit*
6. *Disaster*
7. *Falling Prey to Cruelty of Misfortune*
8. *Revolt*
9. *Daring Enterprise*
10. *Abduction*
11. *The Enigma (temptation or a riddle)*
12. *Obtaining*
13. *Enmity of Kinsmen*
14. *Rivalry of Kinsmen*
15. *Murderous Adultery*
16. *Madness*
17. *Fatal Imprudence*
18. *Involuntary Crimes of Love (example: discovery that one has married one's mother, sister, etc.)*
19. *Slaying of a Kinsman Unrecognized*
20. *Self-Sacrificing for an Ideal*
21. *Self-Sacrifice for Kindred*
22. *All Sacrificed for Passion*
23. *Necessity of Sacrificing Loved Ones*
24. *Rivalry of Superior and Inferior*
25. *Adultery*
26. *Crimes of Love*
27. *Discovery of the Dishonor of a Loved One*
28. *Obstacles to Love*
29. *An Enemy Loved*

30.	*Ambition*
31.	*Conflict with a God*
32.	*Mistaken Jealousy*
33.	*Erroneous Judgment*
34.	*Remorse*
35.	*Recovery of a Lost One*
36.	*Loss of Loved Ones.*

Tobias, Ronald B. 20 Master Plots. Cincinnati: Writer's Digest Books, 1993. This book proposes twenty basic plots:

1.	*Quest*
2.	*Adventure*
3.	*Pursuit*
4.	*Rescue*
5.	*Escape*
6.	*Revenge*
7.	*The Riddle*
8.	*Rivalry*
9.	*Underdog*
10.	*Temptation*
11.	*Metamorphosis*
12.	*Transformation*
13.	*Maturation*
14.	*Love*
15.	*Forbidden Love*
16.	*Sacrifice*
17.	*Discovery*
18.	*Wretched Excess*
19.	*Ascension*
20.	*Descent*

If you're new to writing novels and have no particular ideas, I'd suggest you pick one theme from the above examples and trying running with it! Sometimes being forced to pick a direction is a very quick way of discovering what you don't want to do!

Module Five

Creating Your Novel's Outline

Now we look at a very practical issue: how to structure your novel and create a template from which to construct your novel. I know there are certain writers out there that baulk, spit and pout at the idea of creating an outline for their stories but there's a good reason for doing one, even if only in the roughest form.

The reason is simple.

Having worked closely with hundreds of fiction writers of all types over the last 30 years I can reveal this pertinent fact: 99.99% of all writers who don't start out with a plan for their novels, don't finish them either.

Stressing this point to new writers is actually quite frustrating for me in that nowadays I can usually predict whether an author will finish their book.

It's simple to work out.

If I sense resistance to planning a novel or at least knowing its ending, I can tell the writer will eventually falter. At this point I will usually look skyward, sigh and think, "What a darn shame – another author who won't finish his novel."

It's heart-breaking to know that yet another novel will falter at the quarter point, or three-quarter point (the most common places writers stop) and never see the light of day simply because the author refused to see the benefit of outlining the story.

Let me take a brief moment to explain why novels falter without a plan.

Free-writing is fine for short works. Not having a plan for short stories is okay – as long as you write quickly. Even longer works, say up to 50,000 words may work out without an outline. However, longer works of around 100,000 words and over simply take more time.

And it's the time factor that is crucial. Remember you learned at school that every cell in your body changes within seven years? That, in a sense, every seven years you are a different person?

The same thing is happening to your brain. It is evolving, altering slightly from month to month and therefore, what struck you as a pretty fine idea last year will have flaws for you this year.

This is because you have changed.

You're a different person.

You see things in a different light.

It is for this reason, a novel you started writing for all the right reasons say in January may seem like a less than brilliant idea in October – because by then you've lost that spark, that sense of rightness, that reason why your vision seemed so clear. In simple terms, you're older.

Hence, if you have no plan, no outline to remind you where the story should be heading, it's very easy to get disillusioned by what you're writing and wonder why it seemed so important to begin with.

Suddenly you find your characters aren't behaving as they should. They want to go in different directions.

Why?

Because YOU have changed. YOU feel differently about how your characters should be reacting and how your story is progressing. Not good, or helpful to you as a writer.

You need a plan to hold you on course and keep you focused on the fact that you are not writing a novel in progress. You are writing the novel you PLANNED to write in the first place. And this is ultimately the only kind of novel you will FINISH.

Lecture over. I hope this helps you understand the importance of a novel outline.

Structure

In the last couple of modules we looked at characterization and plotting, more especially how to make sure that your story is logical and that there is a cause and effect for everything in your novel. This is all well and good for the telling of an average story but we're after writing with that little something extra – quality, substance, whatever you want to call it – hence the need for a more concrete structure.

Structure is what gives your story symmetry and depth. It's what will set your novel apart from the many others received by publishers and agents.

But how do we go about it?

Many long term writers find that a sense of good structure comes to them almost automatically. They will have an inbuilt sense of what is right, resulting from years of practice. For the novice, it's more of a process – that can be learned.

Use the template below as your starting point when constructing a novel outline and template.

It's a good idea to complete this template before you start a novel writing session of say, 30 to 90 days. Having the template on hand at all times during your writing sessions will make the writing so much easier - and your novel more manageable.

Fiction 101 – Creating Your Novel Template

Your Story Title:

Your Name (or Pseudonym):

Description of Your Story Line (less than 100 words):

Your Novel's Theme (Message or Moral):

Your Novel's Synopsis (200 to 2000+ words):

Your Novel's Outline (1000 to 20000+ words):

Your Novel's Template:

Relevant Notes:

Necessary Research:

First decide on a working title and place it at the top of the document. Put your name beneath it. Then write a brief description of your story of less than 20 to 50 (max 100) words – a summary if you will, that might appear in a catalogue advertising your book.

Next write down in as few as possible words the theme of your novel, whether it be something as simple as "Love Conquers All" or "Power Corrupts" or perhaps something more specific like "Barney Learns How to Create Happiness From Adversity" or "The Smith Family Triumphs Over Demons From Outer Space". It's important to describe your story to yourself in straightforward terms because the theme (the book's point) must remain your focus, even just subliminally, as you write.

Rather than coming up with a theme, you may decide your novel has a message or moral.

Be careful here not to think in terms of 'preaching'. At all times the good novelist is objective – as an observer and a recorder. If you do have a particular message in mind remember that readers like to see both sides of the argument. They don't want to read a book where the writer seems to have an agenda – unless it is a widely accepted viewpoint like "Good Must Defeat Evil" for instance. Even here, there will be gray areas in some readers' minds.

As a general rule it's best not to 'take a stance' on moral, political or environmental issues as a fiction writer as this may undermine your credibility to a publisher /agent/ editor, and may further undermine your relationship with your eventual reader.

Synopsis

At this point, move on to writing a synopsis of your story. It doesn't matter how rough it is but as a general rule it should display the 'arc' of your story. To simplify this notion for yourself, break the novel into five distinct parts:

1. Introduction – where your characters and their situations are introduced.

2. First slope upwards – where complications and further developments are shown.

3. Continuing slope upwards – where situations and interactions are being pushed to the limit.

4. The apex – where all conflicts and dramas intensify and reach a climax.

5. The gentle down-slope – where the story is resolved and the characters have reached either safety, enlightenment, a point of growth or death.

All good stories more or less follow this age-old structure. If you find that your own story cannot be broken down into these essential elements it may mean you will have to review your plot (created during the last module). You might also need to change the order of events to ensure your story is not meandering or losing its momentum during its telling.

Make sure you have a satisfactory synopsis before you move on to the next stage. Remember that this is an entirely personal judgment. If YOU are satisfied with how your story works at this point in time then, for the purposes of your novel, it works.

Next, if necessary, refine your novel's overriding theme and then move on to the outline.

Outline

Using dot points, short sentences or notes, describe your novel from beginning to end. Don't get too hung up on the details you will need to explain later - during the actual writing.

Keep focused on the necessity to describe ALL of your novel.

I find it helps to write notes for the beginning, the end and the middle in no particular order. Detailing the events and interactions at the end of the story is just as important as the introduction – where, naturally, you might find you are tempted to spend longer because you have more to say. Don't dwell too long on any one section. Get a feel for the whole story.

Make it all work – now, before you move on.

As you write notes, keep your eyes on that theme. Make sure your story, at any point, stays relevant to it.

If you notice sections of the story are not in line with the novel's main theme, you have two options. Re-write the theme to better reflect the story's purpose or delete those sections that do nothing to 'prove' or illustrate the theme or 'point' of your book.

The Template

Once you are happy with your outline for the novel, begin to transfer it, or simpler still, copy and edit it into a working template. Insert chapter headings and structure the events within the chapters to show how your theme is being proved by each successive body of text.

Think of your story as a long series of intellectual 'arguments' that will prove a point to the reader.

In the same way as you might structure a simple sentence to advance a proposition, (in essence this is what writing is all about), then you might structure a paragraph to advance a further, more complex proposition.

The paragraph will therefore contain a subject, its context and the point you want to make. The paragraph will hopefully be logical and guide its reader to information necessary to understand that 'point.'

Your chapter will have much the same purpose. It should be a logical succession of paragraphs that illustrate and explain the point you are trying to make in the story.

Therefore a chapter will have a beginning, middle and end that all go to prove your theme or message (or at least part of the ongoing argument that is your novel).

Finally, your finished story template will be the complete 'argument' that proves, point by point, your theme is true to your reader.

Construct your template with the above guidelines in mind and you won't go far wrong.

The Ending

After the first draft of your novel template, which may be anything between 1000 and 10000 words, take a good look at the ending.

Make sure that all of the story threads are resolved. Also make sure that issues introduced at the end have their roots early on in the story. Make sure that characters and events directly 'responsible' for the novel's ending are (and need to be) foreshadowed early on.

If you find that your ending has little to do with the start of your book, you may well need to start again – at least by going back to the plotting and characterization stage – to ensure you are telling a story that is consistent, purposeful and focused.

The Twist

Story twists are a great way of messing with reader's expectations for entertainment value. However, there are rules. Twists, though unexpected, must always be logical and consistent with what the reader has already been told.

For instance, the true identity of a killer in a mystery or thriller is okay to withhold – as long as there was no way any of the characters (except the killer of course) could have known it before the reader.

Twists must be predictable in the sense that the clues were there for the astute reader. They must be logical except if they are:

Double Twists

This is where a twist is revealed that, if the reader thinks about it, can't be true. The author can then guide the reader back to the 'real' truth that may, of course, be another (believable) twist.

At this point, make sure you do not introduce logic flaws into your manuscript. Sometimes hiding an upcoming twist involves diverting the reader's attention away from it during the story. However, most times doing this can make your entire premise unbelievable.

This is, again, a very good reason for completing an outline first.

Continuity

Make sure your finished template makes total sense – if only to you. By all means get other writers to comment on it if you like. But only make changes if they make sense to you. Don't change little things just because they seem like a good idea at the time.

Always focus on the big view – the whole story and how it works for you – especially at this moment in time.

If you need to, where there are areas you might need to clarify later, make extra notes outside of the template. Also, when it comes to research, make a note of things you will need to look up or gain knowledge about. But remember that you must resolve these issues of research and further notes and finish the template before you move on.

There's nothing worse than getting half way through a novel and realizing a particular plot point doesn't make sense without lots of rewriting. Worse, that a simple piece of research would have told you something couldn't possibly happen – thereby invalidating almost everything you've written to that point!

When you are satisfied your template is complete and proves your point, only then is it time to begin writing that novel. Because by then, you have a potential work of art on your hands. Get to it!

Module Six

Show Don't Tell

This subject is so vitally important to your success (and profitability) as a popular author, it deserves an entire module.

Many writers think they understand the principle of Show Don't Tell but consistently ignore its tenets. Showing and not telling your story is so fundamentally important to modern fiction, you should study this module extensively, especially the examples given, and do the exercises suggested until the concept is firmly implanted in your brain.

What is Meant by "Show Don't Tell?"

Basically, to your readers, it is the difference between being merely told a story and feeling like they are actually there. To passively 'tell' a story is to distance it from the reader, to actively 'show' it is to involve them. There are numerous ways to achieve this.

Reader engagement in fiction is not something that 'better' writers can achieve simply delivering superior prose. No, engagement is achieved by the learned skill of taking the reader into the setting, having them identify with the characters and thereby pulling them into the action and story.

Here's the simplest example I can think of:

Once upon a time there was a princess who lived in a castle with her father, the King.

This is basic storytelling and it's passive – it's telling.

Showing this same information would look something like this:

The princess sat on her bed in the castle. Her father, the King, blustered into the room.

You see the slight difference? The second version has an immediacy the first is lacking. You are there in the room with the characters as opposed to being told about an imaginary scenario.

Okay, you're thinking, but isn't the first version traditionally how authors begin a story? True, we all know that at some point the dialogue will appear and a dragon will start spitting fire. But the technique of beginning stories this way is not favored by modern writers any more because, simply put, it's dull.

Introductions – Sharp or Meandering?

There used also to be a tradition of adult novels starting slowly. Readers would have to wade through two to five pages of passive scene setting, description of everything from the weather, the countryside and the dwellings where the action begins, before they were introduced to, say, a character or two and their situation.

Except in deliberately obtuse literary novels, this is no longer the case. Readers want to pick up a fiction novel and be hauled by the lapels into the story. Hence the need to 'show' right from the beginning, right there in the first paragraph.

Consider this first paragraph:

The morning sun was rising over the Tarquin household as Molly began hauling a fully laden basket toward the washing line.

This kind of writing, even though on the surface would seem to be acceptable, even quite good by a novice writer, is guaranteed to have your story heading for the waste bin (or the rejection pile) before you can say, "Please peruse my manuscript."

Why?

Because its author is making no attempt to engage the reader in this scene. Beautiful, prosaic writing it might be but it's also lazy, self indulgent and, well, ineffectual. More compelling would be:

Molly opened the backdoor to the Tarquin house and squinted at the rising sun. Her breath misted before her face as she hauled the heavy basket toward the washing line.

You see the difference?

Subtle perhaps, but now it's immediate. You're there, with Molly, instead of watching her from some undetermined point in the landscape.

Active versus Passive

In order to write persuasive fiction, you need to keep an eye on which voice you're using: the passive or the active. Writers tend to think that passive writing is somehow more literary because it implies the objectivity required to be considered a 'good' writer. This is in error.

Good writers know that active prose, though perhaps harder to master, is more effective. For example, this is typical of passive writing:

Jake wished everything was different. He hated being in debt. Hated the creditors that pounded on his door in the evenings and the phone calls that made his waking life a misery.

Again, good solid writing but it's also 'telling'. More engaging would be:

Jake screwed up the bill and threw it across his bed-sit toward an overflowing bin. Tears pricked at his eyes and the corners of his mouth involuntarily turned down. Startled, his heart thudded. Was that yet another creditor at the door?

Again, the difference may be subtle – not something a reader might necessarily notice. But it's just as literary, if not more, except that again, with the second version, the reader is there, with Jake, sharing his misery instead of being merely informed of it.

Showing is active. Telling is passive.

Description

Many writers dread writing description. I get asked about how much is enough – or too much – all the time. My answer is always the same: "If you don't like description, then enough is when you're done with it. If you do like it, then it's probably too much."

Okay, so this may sound glib but it's meant without irony.

Too much description can stop a story dead in its tracks.

Description is nowadays employed within popular fiction to serve a purpose: to illustrate and clarify. It is not there to show off your skills as a wordsmith. Many novice writers use descriptive passages as an opportunity to show they can be poetic, seemingly clever and a master of observation. Mistake.

Readers do not want to be dazzled by your prowess with words. They want to enjoy the story you're involving them in. It's very tempting, I know, to write as follows:

Twinkling sunlight danced playfully on the papered wall of his bedroom. Dust motes, unfettered, wafted like mysterious space dust between his eyes and the window pane. An odd, musty smell probed at his nostrils, as though seeking to remind him of something lost, long ago, within the farther reaches of his ailing mind.

Yeah, yeah, yeah. But don't be fooled by the apparent literary nature of this writing. It's not poetic or clever in the context of novel fiction writing. It's bland, self-congratulatory and, let's face it, irritating. More concise, and far more powerful would be:

Tom lay on the bed and smelled death. The sunlight played on his bedroom wall but did little to comfort him. He sighed, wiped his eyes and wished he could remember why he was there.

You see how the second version makes you intrigued about the story? Whereas the first tries only to impress you with lyrical sounding words. As a writer, you might prefer the first – but I'd expect readers to prefer (or at least understand) the second.

Quick Note on Exposition

There's a famous saying: "Writers should never justify or explain their work." I can't recall who said it but I believe it.

Of course this advice is meant to apply to writers after their work is completed. However I've noticed that many novice writers tend to do it DURING their novels. Bad practice.

Way too often, novice writers feel the need to 'fill in' the reader on pertinent information they assume the reader needs to know to understand the story. But just like description, exposition can slow a story down. Most readers prefer to 'shown' the story as it unfolds, scene by scene, rather than have the author stop the flow to explain a few things.

Think in terms of movies. Rarely can a director spend too much time relating back-story to the audience without them wanting to fall asleep or leave the theater.

The next time you notice that your own writing has more than half a page of exposition, consider rewriting it as a series of scenes that show the story rather than tell it. You'll be amazed at how your story seems to suddenly come alive when you do this.

Show Don't Tell and Description

One of the great ways to get around the problems of dealing with description is to use your characters to do it for you. Once you've placed your reader inside the head of a character, their descriptions become less intrusive. Not only do they help the reader visualize the scenes, they tell the reader about the character too. Consider this:

The jungle was a mottled carpet of green beneath the helicopter. It flew for over an hour before it landed on the deserted runway.

This is the omnipresent author describing the scene. Not bad. But surely so much better would be:

Dave looked out of the helicopter window. The jungle was a mottled carpet of green. It seemed to stretch for a million miles during the next hour. Finally, in a space that to Dave thought looked deserted, the helicopter touched down.

You see, again, how, although perhaps less 'literary', the second version takes the reader along with the character. That we're not relying on the author to tell us cold hard facts but we're experiencing the journey with Dave.

Setting

Similarly, instead of describing where your action takes place, have your character do it for you. Just make sure that you stick with one point of view. Remember that stories told by the omniscient author tend to create distance between the reader and the text, like this:

The room was filled with ornate furnishings. Red velvet curtains blocked out the meager sunlight and the large space in the center was dominated by an oak desk.

Not bad, but more engaging would be:

Mason beckoned me into his office. Ornate, antique furnishings everywhere. I noticed heavy red curtains blocked out the meager sunlight. In the center of the room Mason sat behind a large oak desk, eyeing me with suspicion.

Because it's characters that make a story. Without characters' interaction with their environment, descriptions can seem dry and even unnecessary. (I've heard – horror of horrors - some readers skip descriptive passages altogether – to get to the dialogue. Gasp!)

Dialogue

And of course dialogue is the best way to show instead of tell every time, on one condition: that you don't use dialogue to thinly disguise exposition. You know the kind of thing:

"I see young Mary's pregnant again."

"Yep, and her mother's not happy about it."

"I suppose it'll be the rascal Brett who's the father."

Good dialogue draws readers into a story. They find it easy to read and, if the dialogue sounds real, then reader engagement is guaranteed.

Always try to make dialogue as real sounding as possible. Use contractions like don't, can't, won't because that's the way people talk.

Read out your dialogue.

Have your friends read it out to you and notice where they stumble. Listen to them if they tell you your dialogue doesn't sound right. Change it until it flows and sounds natural.

Of course, fictional dialogue is not quite the same as real speech – which is full of hesitations, ums, ers and ahs, and is rarely logical in that people in real life don't usually talk in complete sentences.

But there is a logicality to dialogue – which you'll notice in screenplays and movies if you study them – that you should follow, practice and learn from.

If you're having problems, try writing just dialogue – pages and pages of it if necessary. Imagine two people having an argument and let them at each other. Have one character deliberately take an opposite stance to the other and let them tear each other apart.

When you've done a few pages, read it into a recorder or have a friend help you.

Listen back to it. Is it natural sounding? This is important because in popular modern novels dialogue may make up anything from 30% to 70% of your text.

Conclusion

Whenever you are perusing your writing you need to be critical of your work. It's too easy to think that what you've written is splendid, immutable and profound. This is rarely the case. You must be ready to change whatever isn't perfect. And not feel bad about it.

It's the way of the writer.

Spending 20% of your time writing the first draft and 80% rewriting is not unusual for professional writers. You might think that some authors write beautifully and their prose seems effortless. But this is most times an illusion created by obsessive rewriting.

And don't think that publisher's editors will do it for you. They won't – indeed, your MS is unlikely to get that far if your writing isn't 99% perfect to begin with.

Later, when you're rewriting, keep the idea of 'showing' in mind. Ask yourself, as you write, how can I best show this scene? How can I change a few paragraphs of telling into a scene or two with intros, real time dialogue and lots of conflict and drama?

Do this consistently and you'll notice that even though your writing is filling more pages, the pace will be faster and your story far more compelling.

EXERCISE:

Take the following five 'telling' sentences and create short passages that 'show' the same thing.

1) Terence was cold and didn't feel like staying out.

2) Derek and Jane were sitting at home feeling bored.

3) It was two o clock in the afternoon when Brenda decided to rob the bank.

4) The commanders of Eritrea resigned themselves to defeat at the hands of the Argonauts.

5) The house was old and in need of repair, Jason realized.

Module Seven

The Basics of Writing

This far into the course may seem an odd place to start talking about writing basics but there is good reason for it. It's important to know some simple rules for good writing just *before* you start working on your manuscript - but *after* you've made the decision to begin your novel.

To publishers, pretty much anyone can string a few words together (which of course is part of the problem) but surprisingly few know how to do it properly.

Many would-be successful fiction writers let themselves down by consistently using bad grammar, incorrect punctuation and excessive wordage.

I'm not talking about minor problems that an editor might fix later. Many of the more common writing errors are far too prevalent in new writer's submissions – I know, I see them all the time! It's a great shame because they really do become the difference between the life or death of a manuscript.

You MUST present your writing in its best possible light when it comes to submission time.

Too much fiction is rejected purely because the writing appears incompetent.

I say 'appears' because, with just a little care and attention to detail, most bad habits can be fixed – especially if you learn the rules now, and are mindful of them as you write.

Sentence Construction

The rule is: keep it simple. Don't start out thinking, "I'm going to write beautiful, complex prose that transcends, hypnotizes, inspires" etc. It doesn't work that way. It's the ideas that are important, not the way they are put across.

I sometimes think that good writing can be summed in this one sentence:

The cat sat on the mat.

It contains the subject (the cat), the doing word (or verb, sat) and explains where it took place (the mat). Therefore the sentence has everything necessary for a reader, with no wasted words. It contains the who, what and where of the story, which is all that really matters. You can add adjectives, adverbs and whole load of other words but the basic information doesn't change.

Think of it this way. A sentence is designed to advance a proposition, that is, to 'sell' an argument. A good sentence does this well. An overly complex sentence does it badly – usually because the reader gets lost trying to work out what the subject is (usually the 'who'), what's happening to them and the why/where/when.

Remember that a fiction reader is essentially interested in the story and will attach significance to its events in the following order:

1. *Who*
2. *What*
3. *Where*
4. *When*
5. *Why*
6. *How*

You'll see that, especially in fiction, it's 'Who' that is more important than the other components. Spend too much time writing about the 'Why' and 'How' (the least important components) and the reader will grow restless. To keep a reader involved, focus your story on the top components and edit out too much focus on the lower components.

Remember that you don't have to 'sell' these propositions all at once. Sentences can be short or long but generally, the shorter the better. One or two propositions in one sentence is great. Three is good too but more and you'll tend to confuse the reader.

You're probably getting confused yourself now, so let me give you an example.

Here's a sentence with one proposition:

The gun fired.

Easy to understand. We're given a subject and what happened to it. More engaging would be to know about the 'Who.' So:

Edgar fired the gun.

Still only one proposition but now we've changed the subject to 'Edgar'. More complex now would be:

Edgar fired the gun at Muriel.

Still only one proposition – one fact you want the reader to know. Good, clean simple writing which relates the facts. More complex again:

Edgar fired the gun at Muriel, killing her.

Now we have two propositions – that is two facts we want the reader to know. You see, it's not the number of words that make a sentence harder to grasp, it's the number of propositions you are advancing and expecting the reader to follow. More complex again:

Edgar raised his arm and fired the gun at Muriel, killing her.

Now there are three propositions. This is fine, the reader is still with you. But what surprises me is that many novice writers don't stop here and will begin to add all kinds of extra words, adding complexity for no good reason. For instance:

Gritting his teeth, Edgar tentatively raised his right arm and, briefly closing his eyes, fired the gun which blew Muriel backwards into the wall, killing her, letting her lie in a pool of viscous blood.

Okay, it's OTT but do you see the point? Just because you're adding information, you're not making the writing any better. It's getting worse because in the last sentence there are now EIGHT propositions – in ONE sentence - way too much for a reader to keep up. This is the kind of writing – and sentence construction – you need to avoid.

Keep it simple.

Better would be:

Edgar gritted his teeth and raised his arm. The gun shook in his hand. He closed his eyes and fired; blood spattered as Muriel hit the wall, hard. For a moment Edgar heard only the ringing of gunshot in his ears. Then, he realized, it was over. The woman slumped down to the floor, dead.

You see how using a series of short propositional phrases adds to the drama.

Basically, it's easier to read because the sequence of events is logical, therefore more credible. Plus, it's not encumbered by clumsy grammar. You can use this principle in all kinds of writing from description, exposition to internal dialogue – as long as you keep focusing on the who/what/where and less on the when, why and how, you'll do fine, especially if you consciously try to break down your ideas into short simple sentences along the way.

Punctuation

Far too many new writers fall down when it comes to punctuation, it's worth taking time out to study it – indeed, even if you're a full time professional, it's easy to make the odd mistake.

The use of commas and speech marks seem to be an especially common problem.

Commas are most effective when they are used to separate propositions.

Secondarily, they may be used to denote a pause or rest (although this fashion is declining.)

Speech marks (obviously) are used to denote dialogue. In the US, double speech marks denote normal speech but in the UK and Australia, single speech marks are the norm.

To avoid confusion, most publishing houses prefer to use italics to denote internal dialogue or, for instance, lines from songs etc, but there is still some disagreement as to whether a writer should use underlining to mean italics in MSS.

I think if it was up to writers, italics should mean you want the word italicized (not bolded, as it means to printers) simply because it's more logical. My partner, mindful of these issues, doesn't use italics/underlining in her MSS at all. It's a good test of your work.

If you can get a point across without underlining/italicizing or emboldening words, your prose is probably more effective.

BTW: Don't use capitals to denote emphasis in fiction. Ever. Similarly, avoid exclamation marks, especially when using them to denote humor or irony.

Commas and speech marks combined are a common problem area too, especially when dealing with where to capitalize. For instance, these are correct:

Jake said, "Give me that."

(Note the comma comes before the speech and the first word of dialogue is capitalized.)

"Give me that," said Jake.

(Note the comma is inside the speech marks.)

"Give me that," said Jake, "so I can use it."

Or, more often:

"Give me that," said Jake. "I want to use it."

Breaks in speech require the em-rule, a solid line, and not ellipses (three dots), as in:

"Hey, sister, don't make me—"

Try to avoid using ellipses at all. To many writers they signify a pause – usually in their thinking. They're more effective when implied rather than used.

Also, commas are utilized to separate out names in dialogue, as in:

"You know what I want, Dave."

Or,

"Dave, you know what I want."

The same is true for terms like Mum, darling, sweetie, mate or whatever.

A quick note. Contrary to 'conventional' wisdom, a semicolon is not 'half way between a comma and a colon'.

Semi-colons have a specific purpose: to separate items on a list. They are most times interchangeable with commas and many publishing houses remove them as a matter of course. Tip? Don't use them.

Remember that the idea of fiction writing is to transfer your ideas/images into the head of a reader. Failure to apply the accepted conventions of punctuation means that the reader 'trips' over your mistakes and 'selling your proposition' becomes so much harder for you.

If you're unsure, study paperbacks. Look at the punctuation, analyze it. Learn from it.

Style

Many new writers are confused about style. What is it? And where are we supposed to find it – or get one? This is to misunderstand what is meant by 'style'.

Style has two components. One is to do with everything we've looked at so far in this module. It's about knowing the rules first, before you decide to break them.

Later, style is personal. It's about the way you see the world and how your mind processes information. Especially how you process information via your writing.

Ideally you want to reach a position whereby what you write reflects the way you think – otherwise writing will always be hard for you. This is often why novice writers get stuck – they're not writing in their own style, they're yet to understand how their individual mind works.

There's no real short cut. Attaining a style comes from writing. The more you do it, the more your style becomes honed, over time, word by word. However, by learning the basic rules of good punctuation and grammar, you can arrive at a style more quickly than by sticking with what you think you know.

For instance, there's no point continually making grammatical errors and saying, "Well, that's just my style," because this is to misunderstand the concept of 'writing style'.

Your style grows out of your need to clarify your thoughts, your personal sense of logic, based on the accepted writing conventions. Not on breaking rules because you don't know them!

Most professional, long-term writers I know are still fascinated by all the little nuances of punctuation and grammar; whether to use contractions, dots between acronyms; how to write dates, numbers in text; all the little things that might seem petty.

Because, to a good writer, these things aren't petty: they are the tools that help refine and define their style.

So, if you think the 'rules' aren't important, think again!

Here's a famous list of 'the rules'. It's meant to be humorous because it shows the mistakes as well as drawing attention to them. It's worth studying – and if you don't find it funny, or don't get it, you need to seriously question your commitment to writing!

- Avoid run-on sentences they are hard to read.
- Don't use no double negatives.
- Use the semicolon properly, always use it where it is appropriate; and never where it isn't.
- Reserve the apostrophe for it's proper use and omit it when its not needed.
- Do not put statements in the negative form.
- Verbs has to agree with their subjects.
- No sentence fragments.
- Proofread carefully to see if you any words out.
- Avoid commas, that are not necessary.
- If you reread your work, you will find on rereading that a great deal of repetition can be avoided by rereading and editing.
- A writer must not shift your point of view.
- Eschew dialect, irregardless.
- And don't start a sentence with a conjunction.
- Don't overuse exclamation marks!!!
- Place pronouns as close as possible, especially in long sentences, as of ten or more words, to their antecedents.
- Hyphenate between sy-llables and avoid un-necessary hyphens.
- Write all adverbial forms correct.
- Don't use contractions in formal writing.
- Writing carefully, dangling participles must be avoided.
- It is incumbent on us to avoid archaisms.
- If any word is improper at the end of a sentence, a linking verb is.
- Steer clear of incorrect forms of verbs that have snuck in the language.
- Take the bull by the hand and avoid mixed metaphors.
- Avoid trendy locutions that sound flaky.
- Never, ever use repetitive redundancies.
- Everyone should be careful to use a singular pronoun with singular nouns in their writing.
- If I've told you once, I've told you a thousand times, resist hyperbole.
- Also, avoid awkward or affected alliteration.
- Don't string too many prepositional phrases together unless you are walking through the valley of the shadow of death.
- Always pick on the correct idiom.

- "Avoid overuse of 'quotation "marks."'"
- The adverb always follows the verb.
- Last but not least, avoid clichés like the plague; seek viable alternatives

I hope this module helps you understand some of the challenges associated with presenting good manuscripts.

It's by no means a full treatise on the subject – that would take a book or three.

But I hope it's enough to at least alert you to the importance of getting things right in your writing, before you let too many bad habits creep into your work.

Of course, there are lots of ways to express yourself in the English language and not all of the rules are set in stone.

Use of language should be organic, and reflect the people who use it.

I believe that breaking the rules is fine, and many times effective, but you should ideally know the rules first.

Module Eight

Scene Structure, Exposition and Setting

Scene structure is rarely covered in fiction writing courses. I think this is because it's assumed that most writers must have an innate way of expressing themselves – and that scene structure is somehow too personal to teach.

Whilst this may be true to some extent, scene structure is important – particularly in screenplay writing – where scene structure is the heart of the movie. And, given that the best novels nowadays can often go on to become screenplays and movies, then learning from screenplay writing can be valuable to the modern fiction writer.

Many bestselling writers nowadays write scenes in novels as though they are designed to go straight to film. Writers like Michael Chrichton, James Patterson, Dan Brown and JK Rowling write using well tested movie making techniques for creating scenes in their fiction.

So, how are scenes constructed in modern scriptwriting?

In movies, scenes are generally constructed like this:

1. Short establishing shot of the setting
2. A compelling opening
3. Brief exposition (optional)
4. The focal point
5. Ensuing drama

6. Additional exposition (optional)

7. A hook

You can immediately see that in movies, there are rules. There is also very little room for maneuver. No time is wasted and the ideas must be crystal clear.

Studying movie scenes can also help you with discipline. Because it's a ruthless business and, if a movie works without a scene, it will be dropped. After all, there's no real point relating information that does little to advance the story.

Of course, novels can work on a more cerebral level. The advantage with scenes in novels is that you, the author, can add internal thoughts and background information that the filmmaker cannot. This can add depth to your prose and characterization. However, it may also hinder a scene in that it can slow down the action.

I believe the best way to teach scene construction is by example. I hope the examples below will help you in this regard. As always, I'll be trying to keep it easy to understand, even simplistic, so that you can grasp the basics and augment as you see fit.

Scene Structure

At its most basic level a scene in a novel is designed to convey information about the plot. Either to show an important event or change in the character's actions or motivations.

When planning a scene you need to decide on the Focal Point – that is the particular piece of information (or pieces of information) you want to convey.

First, write your Focal Point(s) down, in shorthand if you like. It's important to know the 'point' of a scene before you start, otherwise you'll find that your writing lacks direction.

But this is not enough in itself. You also have a responsibility to make a scene as interesting, entertaining or compelling as possible. There's a simple rule to follow here:

Start big and end with a cliffhanger.

This is not to say every scene must have intergalactic forces warring over planets. There are far more subtle ways of starting big and ending with a cliffhanger – your personal interpretation is important so long as you remember not to meander through scenes as though you had all the time in the world, or feel the necessity to tell every little detail and nuance of it. For instance:

Focal point: Geoff meets with Sandra for advice.

Sample opening:

Geoff didn't know what to do. He ran a hand over the stubble on his chin and tilted the rear view mirror to check his appearance. His bloodshot eyes stared back at him accusingly. He hoped Sandra didn't get too close — he was sure last night's tequila was still on his breath.

This is a compelling opening to a scene because the reader is asking questions.

What is it that Geoff needs to do? Why is he hung-over? What will Sandra make of him? And who is Sandra anyway?

All this is pulling your reader into the story.

Next you might describe the meeting with Sandra, have them exchange dialogue to deal with the Focal Point. Then end with something cryptic or engaging, like this:

Sandra digested the facts and seemed on the point of speaking when, bang, a gunshot rang out upstairs.

When it comes to writing modern novels the important thing is not to waste words, especially at the beginning of scenes. Many writers are tempted to do this because they feel 'setting the scene' is a nice way of guiding readers into their stories. This is largely unnecessary, mainly because readers are used to being pulled into scenes very quickly in TV dramas and movies. Just a few words will be enough in most cases to set the scene.

Quite often nowadays, the scene is set AFTER the compelling opening.

For instance:

Lizzy noticed the car — that distinctive blue Chevy — was parked across the street again. Her eyes scanned the rundown shops and offices of Mercantile Place. She wasn't sure what she was looking for. Strange men in black? Bug-eyed aliens?

Another example:

The detective knew this day would be trouble. It was five o'clock in the morning and a pale sun was beginning to rise over Boston.

What you must try to avoid is bland openings that don't compel the reader to read on, like this:

Rita opened the muesli box and poured herself a generous helping. As she chewed on her breakfast, she gazed at the sycamore tree blooming outside of her kitchen window. Birds chirruped gaily, a dog barked somewhere in the distance...

Okay, this 'sets the scene' but does it pull you in sufficiently?

Is the writer trying hard enough to engage your interest?

Or is he merely filling in time before the action starts?

At this point the average reader might be thinking, Will there ever be any action if the story starts like this?

Most likely the reader won't bother to read on. A publisher wouldn't, that's for sure.

Always remember that there must by a POINT to your scenes. Just because you can string a few words together doesn't mean you are necessarily creating compelling fiction.

This is a mistake many unpublished writers make. It's not enough to be able to write well – you also have to be aware of your reader at all times. Strive to intrigue and entertain them, not with pretty sounding words but with STORY.

Start a scene in the heat of the action / drama / focal point (or as close to it as you can) and fiercely edit out any extraneous writing – no matter how well executed – that doesn't pull the reader along with the plot.

Scene Transition

It's tempting to describe events and character's actions in between important scenes. There is generally not to be advised. Think again in terms of movies. Would the film director need to show a character eating meals, driving or bathing if it's not integral to the plot? Of course not. Most times it's wise to 'cut' to the scenes that only further the story.

In novels it's perfectly acceptable to jump from one place to another with little or no explanation. Sometimes just a few words is enough to orientate the reader, especially if the ending of the previous scene makes it clear where the next piece of action will most likely take place.

Exposition (Again)

Of course pacing is important. Sometimes it's good to slow the action in a novel down to give the reader time to breathe – or fill in some of the blanks in the storyline. A good way to do this is through exposition.

Exposition is basically background information that allows the reader to understand the context of the story and more fully identify with its characters.

It's important to use exposition sparingly. It's hard to generalize but more than 1000 words of back-story / explanations of motivations etc is probably too much for a novel aimed at the average reader. Exposition most times is fairly static, so you risk boring the reader when you're probably trying to do the opposite.

Plus, readers don't particularly like having a story 'explained' to them. They prefer to be involved with the characters and 'get' the story as they go along.

Whenever you're faced with large amounts of prose that is mainly 'telling' your story, try breaking down the text into extra scenes that 'show' the information instead. This will help remove passive writing and create a more colorful and energetic manuscript.

Action versus Dialogue

Again, it's hard to generalize because the proportion of action to dialogue is such a personal matter. However, you should know that readers, in general, prefer dialogue. Some publishers, particularly romance houses, even state that anywhere between 50% to 70% dialogue is what their readers prefer.

Setting

Often referred to as the 'other' character, setting can do much to bring your MS to life. Using specific locations, real or otherwise, can add veracity and color to your stories.

In real life people feel grounded in the places they live. Giving your main characters a sense of attachment with their home can help reader identification.

Think of Stephen King and Castle Rock and Maine immediately

spring to mind. In fact King uses the idiosyncrasies of the geography and the people that live there to augment his horror themes – to make them more believable.

Patricia Cornwell's Kaye Scarpetta famously lives in Richmond, Virginia.

Kathy Reichs sets her stories in Canada (though not on TV.)

And where else could the Rumpole stories, or Sherlock Holmes, be set other than London?

Don't be afraid to use real locations. Robert Ludlum spends much of his time traveling, collecting maps and photographing towns, streets, buildings (as does Dan Brown) to ensure their settings are portrayed accurately (within a fictional context.)

Writers often ask me if it's okay to use real places in fiction. Of course it is, as it's also okay to use real people and real products and real events. Even real organizations.

Your only proviso is that you cannot deliberately offend people, groups, places or companies. Well, you can if you want to – if you don't mind being sued!

Environments

Writers have an odd tendency to believe that anywhere is a good setting but the place they live. I suppose we get used to where we are and fail to see how glamorous or intriguing it may seem to an outsider.

Generally I believe (and some agents I know disagree with me) that your home location is probably the best setting for your stories. Mainly because researching other locations you're not familiar with is hard work – and easy to mess up. The last thing you want is, for instance, your character to catch a bus in a particular location only to find out later, the place has no bus service.

For many of my own stories I use a fictional town called Westbridge – or sometimes West Ridge – because I can add to it as I see fit. I also use places I visit, like Cambodia, Greece and London – especially if the protagonist is a tourist in those places.

My most recent novel is set in Adelaide, Australia – because that's where I live and I also feel compelled to let outsiders know what this city is like (at least to me.)

But at the end of the day, it's up to you. Much of everything actually is up to you in fiction. As I often say, there are many rules, which you should study and learn from. But, when you know those rules, you're a prime position to break them.

Module Nine

Structuring Chapters

Last module we looked at scene structure and how to focus on pivotal points in your story to best effect. This module we look at chapter structure, and how best to organize your story within the context of a novel.

You'll remember a few modules back that I said that a fiction novel is basically a series of propositions that you are 'selling' to a reader. In general terms these are:

1. Let me introduce my characters – they are real.

2. Let me tell you what happened to them – it's all true.

3. Stick with me and you'll be entertained, informed and/or learn a lesson.

In return, your reader suspends their disbelief while reading and 'buys' into your world, accepting your propositions – but only if you present a convincing 'argument' for them. And it's how to best structure that 'argument' that this module chiefly concerns.

Chapter Structure

How long you make your average chapter is of course a personal issue. As short as 800 words is enough for some and up to 5000 to 12,000 is appropriate for others. It depends largely on how much information you want to impart within the chapter that's important.

James Patterson's books have an average of 150 chapters. That's because he likes to impart only one significant plot point in each chapter. Most authors will include between 5 and 10 plot points in a chapter. As a general guide, a new plot point for every 1000 words would be about right for the average genre novel. In children's fiction, a new plot point every 100 words would be more the norm.

So, when you're looking at your novel outline, decide how many plot points you want to group together: one, two, five, ten, whatever, and think of them as groups of ideas that will become a chapter.

Then decide on what the theme of the chapter might be. Where it sits within the novel will be a deciding factor in this process. For instance, your overall story arc might look like this:

1. Characters and their dilemmas, goals, obstacles

2. Ensuing developmental drama

3. Elevated developmental drama

4. Crisis points

5. Conclusion

You might then further break down the novel structure in this way:

1. Characters and their dilemmas, goals, obstacles

Chapter 1

Chapter 2

Chapter 3

2. Ensuing developmental drama

Chapter 4

Chapter 5

3. Elevated developmental drama

Chapter 6

Chapter 7

Chapter 8

4. Crisis points

Chapter 9

Chapter 10

Chapter 11

5. Conclusion

Chapter 12

Each chapter then, depending on its place within the novel, will serve a specific purpose. Chapter 1, for example, might introduce Todd, his desire to be an airline pilot and the obstacles to that dream. This will become the theme of Chapter 1. Take, say, five plot points from your outline that will emphasize this theme and list them:

Chapter 1 – Introduction of Todd
    Scene 1 – Todd at science museum, ogling planes
    Scene 2 – Todd meets father, who doesn't approve, they argue
    Scene 3 – Todd meets Mandy, girlfriend, who dumps him
    Scene 4 – Todd needs to be alone, finds a park
    Scene 5 – Todd dreams of his ambition, makes a silent vow

You do this because you want your chapters to have an over-arcing theme. Plus, it's easier to write when you know specifically what you're trying to prove – this holds true for any piece of writing.

Focus

It's easy to get lost when you're writing a novel. Mainly because you want to put everything into your writing – every nuance, every subtlety, every piece of genius that is you. However, do this and your writing will quickly become dense, hard to follow and even painful to read. To counter, you need to stay focused – not on you, the writer and his writing, but on the story. Remember that what you leave out of your writing is just as important, perhaps even more so, than what you leave in.

Hemingway was perhaps one of the first modern novelists to observe this phenomenon. He said that when you write about what you know, the reader somehow gets it and doesn't require you to describe everything – they fill in the blanks themselves because they trust you and your vision.

Conversely, if you over-explain, over describe and over compensate, the reader loses faith – the reader feels you're writing to convince yourself, rather than the reader – and doesn't believe what you're describing is real anymore.

This is something to bear in mind later, when you're editing, but it's also helpful now, before you begin writing. People often tell me they get stuck writing certain passages and this in turn stops them writing at all – a symptom of writer's block. My advice is, if you're having trouble writing a section, leave it out and move on because it probably doesn't need to be there anyway!

Your focus should be on the story you want to tell, not the need to follow conventions that say, oh, you need some description here or, darn, I need some internal dialogue here etc. Generally, if you think you should put something in but you can't raise the enthusiasm to write it, forget about it. Because when you force writing – somehow the reader gets that it's forced too.

Keeping Your Reader Engrossed

Maintaining a reader's interest in your story has as much to do with structure as it has with the actual text.

Say you have a story about three characters, John, Jane and Suzy. John is the main protagonist. Too much focus on Jane and Suzy will throw your story off kilter. You see this all the time. Writers will say, Oh, well the character took over – she had so much to say. Before you know it, you're writing a different story. That's fine but, if this happens to you, you will need to go back and re-structure the story before you move on. Because if you don't, you'll get stuck later. Trust me on that one.

Pacing is about knowing when you've told the reader enough about one aspect of a story, and deciding when to move on. Too much focus on back-story or plot exposition will have the same effect. You need to be aware of balance. And balance is what you're trying to achieve in your outline, your scene structure and your chapter structure.

It comes down to the clarity of your vision.

It could be you're a genius – or you've written a hundred stories – and that you need make no plans. You just write and somehow everything falls into place. The pacing, drama and tension are all there in the right measure and the story blows people's socks off. Great but, over the course of an 80000 word novel, can you really expect this to happen spontaneously? You'd need huge faith in your mind and abilities to believe this.

Besides, that's doing it the hard way. Juggling the entire plot of your novel in your head is just too much for the average writer. Much better that the balance is achieved first, on paper, in the form of an outline that is broken down scene by scene, chapter by chapter, act by act.

Vision and Structure

Your vision should be reflected in your story structure. You need specific plot points to anchor your story. Try this analogy:

Imagine your story as a piece of rope hanging between two poles a mile apart. Clearly, when the wind blows the rope will swing and sway back and forth, high and low and from side to side. This is a story that lacks direction, one where the reader will be seesawing with the vagaries of an unstructured plot.

Now imagine that every one hundred yards you erect another pole and hitch the rope to it, over its entire length. Here is a story that is structured, where specific points are held and proved in a logical and linear way. This is the kind of story that a reader will enjoy – because now it's focused, on course and more satisfying to read.

A Word of Caution

It's almost funny. Whenever I stress the importance of structuring a novel chapter by chapter, I invariably receive homework exercises that try to break the rules – as if this were inherent in the activity.

Time lines are more often than not deliberately disrupted. Past and future events are told simultaneously. Seemingly unrelated characters take centre stage in alternate chapters. People become animals, ghosts, or talismans. The list goes on. I guess it's because writers feel the need to be original…

However, messing with a story structure should not be your goal in this exercise. For one thing, messing with time lines, POV and novel structure is NOT particularly original. Every author tries it at least once, usually later in their career – when they're more competent. But this kind of writing is not what is required of the first time author.

Your job is to prove to a publisher you know how to tell a good, linear story first and foremost. Messing with structure marginalizes the appeal of your book, placing in the realms of 'literary fantasy' which, by the way, is not a genre publishers actively seek.

So, be kind to yourself. Make your job easier and use structuring as a tool to help you write your novel more easily, more surely and without stress.

Which is what we're studying next module: the actual writing of your novel. How to write quickly and easily with confidence and self belief. How to keep going when the going gets tough. How to stay in control of your drama, dialogue, exposition and especially your reader's attention. Most of all, how to stay focused for long enough to actually FINISH your novel – at least the all important first draft.

You may be thinking that at this point in this book we've spent quite a long time on preparation. This is deliberate. I believe, based on the many years I've spent studying writers and their fiction, that adequate preparation is the skeleton key that unlocks the writer's ability to create the best and most sellable novels.

But, of course, there's only one sure fire piece of advice you need to succeed at writing and that is to keep writing!

□□

Module Ten

Writing Your Manuscript

The most important facet of writing a manuscript is commitment. Not just to work on it consistently but to commit right from the beginning to FINISH it.

So many writers stumble on this point. They're happy to write, enjoying the process, but with no clear end in sight. They know it will take them some time to write a novel but they're not sure how long. The end date keeps extending until they realize five years has gone by. Ten years. Twenty years. And they still haven't finished their book.

They go through all kinds of angst. Wondering over their talent. Questioning it. Contemplating it. All to naught.

Wondering whether your writing is any good is irrelevant when it comes to manuscript production. The whole MS is the thing – the tone of it, the rhythm of it, your way with words is primarily defined when, and only when, it is finished.

You simply can't know how good a MS is, or how good you are as a writer, until it's done. So, by far the most important decision you have to make before you start writing, is to write until it's over. And that's about planning.

Planning

Each time you decide to write a manuscript, you need to work out how long it will take you and how much time you are going to set aside for it. The key to this is word count. You need to know, on average, how many words you can write in an hour.

Contrary to what most people think, full time writers don't spend hours staring at a blank screen or typing their opening sentences over and over again. If they did, they would never produce any manuscripts. No, writers write or, as John Braine once said, writers count words.

For instance, I'm working on a novel at the moment. I'm pretty busy with other stuff so I decided to set aside just a little time – with the help of my partner. It's only four hours a week, not much I know, but this was all I could afford to give it. The alternative was not to write fiction at all and use the time to do something that would bring in money more immediately. But my partner insisted. She has great faith in my fiction and doesn't believe I spend enough time on it.

So anyway, four hours we decided was enough to at least produce something.

Now, I write every day – letters, assessments, emails, lessons, newsletters, promos, non fiction books, whatever. But I can only afford to spend two hours on Monday and Tuesday evenings, between seven and nine, to write fiction. There's not much on TV at these times and if there is, we can always tape it.

I write roughly 1000 words an hour. That might sound like a lot but remember this is 'first draft' writing. I'm just writing as fast as my brain works, getting down the words as they occur to me. Also remember that I work to my outline, so I don't have to think about what happens next – I've already done that. I use the outline to prompt me and when I run out of things to say, I move on to the next 'prompt' in the outline and work on that.

Working this way I produce around four thousand words a week. I'm guessing my novel will be around 80000 words so, with a little help from a calculator (I was never very good at math) I know I will finish the first draft of the novel within 20 weeks. Not bad, eh?

You must do the same. Work out when you're going to write and for how long. Then work out how many words you can write and from that work out how long you will take to write your novel. Then make it a goal to finish your novel within that time. Write down the goal, mark out the time on a calendar and spend a few minutes promising yourself you will do it. Make the commitment – say it out loud, at least once a week.

Writing Without Stopping

Right now, I'm going to prove to your that I'm psychic. Because I know exactly what you're thinking. Your thinking, yeah, that's alright for you, but…

Am I right?

Your thinking, yeah, I would love to set aside time like that, I would love to be able to write that many words, but my life isn't like that. I never know what I'm doing from one moment to the next, let alone on a daily or weekly basis… and even if I could write 1000 words an hour, they probably wouldn't be any good…

How do I know this is what you're thinking? Because I used to be same. Plus, it's something would-be writers tell me all the time.

The fact is it doesn't matter how fast you write. If you write only 100 words at a time, that's still better than nothing. A lot better. If you can only write for a few minutes every now and then, that's still better than not at all.

But you must make the commitment to write. You owe it to yourself.

Wilbur Smith says he writes 500 words a day. It takes him an hour or so, sometimes a lot less. But that means, even if he only works weekdays and takes off all the public holidays and weekends, he's still producing a 125,000 word book a year.

Getting In The Mood

Another common excuse for not writing is waiting until you feel inspired or 'in the right mood'. This is a mistake. You've heard the phrase: "Success is 1% inspiration and 99% perspiration." The same is true for writing. If you wait until you're inspired to write, you'll probably wait a very long time – perhaps forever.

It doesn't matter how you feel, just write. And if you don't feel inspired, fake it. It will come.

And when you're writing it's as well to remember that you should never question your abilities. This is a trick I learned early on. Self doubt is the major killer of creativity. Self doubt should be banished from your mind at all costs. Of course, this doesn't necessarily make you a great writer but it does at least make you a writer – a producer of words.

Write Without Thinking

You should be writing with the creative side of your brain. The other side of your brain is the logical half, the critical half that will halt you and make you question what you write. Whenever you think you're analyzing your writing and finding it wanting, banish those thoughts. Just write, write without stopping – this will usually keep your logical, rational, critical side at bay. And as I say, don't question your abilities, just write and keep writing.

Don't worry about the mechanics – the words, the sentences, and so on, until after you have the bare bones down. Writing is one thing, editing is another. Don't combine these activities – it doesn't favor productivity.

How to Stay on Target

Dream. Dream big. Dream about all the great and good things that will happen to you when you're a best-selling author. Fantasize about how good you will feel when you've finished your novel. How great you will feel when you start submitting it. And how fabulous it will be to get it excepted for publication, or get the movie deal. These are the things that give your manuscript project 'legs' and help maintain your motivation. These are the things that will inspire you to keep writing, even when you don't feel like it. It's okay to feel these things. It's okay to dream.

Who's Leading Your Story?

Many writers tell me they get stuck over their characters. Either sub characters take over the story or main characters run out of things to say and do. I read many manuscripts where minor characters are overly developed to the detriment of the story.

It's all about focus – and sticking to your outline. New and interesting characters are fun – but if you find they're taking over, cut back on their influence and save the ideas for another manuscript.

Writing Out of Corners

Stephen King says he doesn't use outlines – or rather he did once on *The Dead Zone*, and didn't like it! He says he deliberately puts his characters into impossible situations and then tries to get the out of them by using the tenacity of the characters rather than manipulating the plot. This the right way to do it.

Many writers realize they're in a hole and stop writing only to fret and wonder what went wrong. However, nothing went wrong. All you have to do is keep writing and work yourself out of the hole with words. Not thought. Not pondering the universe outside you window. By simply writing.

Getting Past the 'Two-Thirds' Slump

Many writers feel discouraged and / or near to exhaustion at the 2/3rds point in their novel. This is mainly because the bulk of the work is done. But there seems to be such a long way to go to complete a vision that perhaps you're beginning to see holes in. Fight this feeling.

Use the same energy to finish the MS that you used at the beginning. If it's hard to keep going, fake it, keep going anyway. You'll find that you'll feel renewed energy when you've finished the first draft. And that's good – because you're going to need it – for the editing!

Module Eleven

The Editing Process

Writing the First Draft - So it's Finally Over?

Finishing the entire first draft of a novel can be an exhausting and curiously unsatisfying experience. There's something about writing the last line of a novel that is anti-climactic, a far cry from the passion and urgency you felt at the manuscript's outset.

But this is fine, to be expected. Don't fret or lose any sleep over it.

Understandably loathe to let your book go, you may feel tempted to begin the journey all over again, right from the start, with the editing process.

Don't. At least not for a while – at least 6 weeks, if not twice that. Find something else to do, a new project to begin, something else to write.

You need distance from your manuscript. It's nigh on impossible to know what is right or wrong, good and bad about your manuscript while it is still so fresh in your mind. This is because you're still inside it. If you try to edit too soon, your mind fills in the blanks for you while you're reading. You forget to include details because you assume they're already there. You leave in passages because you like them – even though they do nothing to help the story.

You need to come back and read your manuscript later, like an outsider – to read it with fresh eyes, just as your reader will do, someday soon.

You need to completely let go, which is why getting involved in another, equally engrossing project is the best way forward for you. You literally need to flush your first draft out of your system.

Imagine you're the RAM chip in your computer. When you turn off a computer, all of the operating instructions and data within the RAM are expunged, drained away – to be replaced next time you boot up the computer. Do the same thing with your mind – expunge the manuscript from it. Wipe it clean. Start fresh.

Editing

For most professional writers this is fairly intensive process. And not to be taken lightly. Good editing is what separates the wannabes from the gonnabes. It's what defines whether your novel is publishable – so you need to take editing very seriously.

This is how it's done:

First off, you need to read the manuscript through quickly, fixing obvious typos and marking areas that may need extra work or passages that may need deleting.

Then, starting from page one, look at each sentence in turn. Does it make sense? Is it grammatically correct? Is it easy to read and understand? Is there a better way of phrasing it?

Don't rush. This is not a race. Each line is as important as every other line. Be diligent. Make sure you're happy with each sentence before you move on.

Remove unnecessary adverbs and adjectives. Be conscious of the rhythm of the words but don't over-poeticize. Fiction is not poetry. Too much lyricality and your reader may be lulled into sleep, while overuse of too many staccato sentences will jar. Try to strike a good balance. Make the prose flow naturally.

Read each sentence over and over – aloud if you like – to ensure it's not too long, complicated or difficult to read. Checking a sentence in this way half a dozen, a dozen times, is not unusual for the professional writer. To be less thorough is being cavalier with your readers.

Next, look at the flow of the sentences. Is it logical? Are you connecting facts, information and story in a coherent way? Look for other ways to interpret what you're saying. Are there phrases or passages that readers might misinterpret? Can you re-write them so that there's no confusion, no question as to what you mean?

The object of this exercise is to make your writing appear effortless. Ironically perhaps, it is the process of ruthlessly editing text that makes it appear it was written in one sitting. Ponder that – it's an important lesson to learn.

Then look at the flow of your scenes. Have you included enough setting, characterization, dialogue? Is there too much? Are there paragraphs you could delete without harming the story? There's no right or wrong way when it comes to making these decisions. It's simply a matter of doing what you feel is right for the story. What feels right to you.

As an aside: I've found that when I'm having trouble phrasing a sentence or paragraph – whether it's just to do with construction or tone of voice, I often delete the whole thing, just to see what the text looks like without it. Many, many times, the text is improved and no real sense is lost – quite the opposite sometimes!

Over Editing

After a ruthless edit of the original manuscript it's possible that the text may appear to become a little lifeless. This doesn't necessarily mean that it is. It just means that everything that has a potential to jar has been removed, which is good.

However, you may find that the addition of the odd word or two might help the flow, even though technically they might not be necessary. Again, it's a matter of personal taste. Be conscious of the sound of your own voice when reading through the later edits of your material and if, for instance, you continually stumble over words that, although technically correct, don't sound natural to you, don't be afraid of inserting punctuation, words and phrases to help the flow.

There's a famous funny story about Oscar Wilde, who was once working on a manuscript while staying with a friend.

"So, what have you been doing this morning, Oscar?" asked his friend.

"After much thought, I decided on deleting a comma," Mr. Wilde said.

"You mean to tell me," the outraged friend countered. "You've spent the last four hours writing in your room and all you did was delete a comma?"

"Of course not," said Mr. Wilde seriously. "In the end I decided to put it back in again."

To me, this is a joke that only writers will fully understand. It underlines just how fastidious a good writer should be.

Rewriting

At any stage in the editing process you should be prepared for a little rewriting.

As you go through your manuscript be aware of pacing. Try to strike an even balance between dialogue and exposition. Remember to show and don't tell too often.

Look for flaws in the logic, especially in your characters' motivations and actions. Don't be afraid to deal with these issues with the addition of explanations, internal dialogue and extra scenes.

But most of all, keep in mind that your reader is reading for pleasure – to be entertained and taken out of themselves. Your first responsibility is to your reader.

Help with Editing

If you're new to editing, it's a good idea to have another competent writer help you. There are many good practices that you may be lacking in your arsenal. Ignorance is no excuse. What may be perfect to you may still be full of fundamental flaws. Experience has shown me that many new writers continue to make the same errors for years unless corrected early on. Don't be afraid to ask someone with experience to peruse your work and help you with the technical side of writing: basic grammar, punctuation and the 'rules' as we discussed in an earlier module.

However, editing for style is different.

Others may suggest you're lacking certain elements or overly dwelling on other aspects. Listen to them, consider their views but, if it doesn't make absolute sense to YOU, don't act on their suggestions. Whatever you do, don't hack your writing around to please others – including publishers and agents. Because if the final manuscript doesn't ultimately work for you, it won't work for anyone else.

When publishers and agents make suggestions for improvements, they often don't mean what they say, I've noticed. I've witnessed many writers reworking their material to fulfill the expectations of publishers in particular only to be rejected when they submit the new work. This is so common a phenomena as to be worthy of a brief study.

There are several issues at play here, I think.

First off, let's face it, if publishers knew what was needed in a good manuscript, they would be writers themselves. Most are not. Many are failed writers.

Secondly, when they suggest revisions, publishers are using their own subjective judgment which, even they themselves don't particularly trust – especially when they're shown what their ideas look like in black and white.

Thirdly, I believe that when a publisher says you need this, that and the other in your MS, what they're really saying is, "Show me something better," which, of course, requires a whole different methodology to merely rewriting what you have.

When it comes to rewriting for publishers and agents, I believe the message is clear: *Trust Your Own Instincts.*

Having said that, be rigorous with your own writing. Consider it from every viewpoint. Be prepared to hate it sometimes. Really work on improving it – even when you think it's perfect. Writing is never perfect. It's a fluid medium that can be manipulated right up to the point of publication. This is okay. It doesn't undermine your talent.

You need to accept the idea that your words are mere tools used to convey your ideas. How ideas come across is flexible, organic – and resistance to change is the way of the amateur. Professionals know that, though the words matter, they are not necessarily set in stone.

Another Aside: NEVER send publishers, agents or other

important personages unfinished drafts. It doesn't matter how much you stress the work is unfinished, needs polishing etc, you will always be judged on what is seen. Better – always – to make them wait than stop your career in its tracks. And believe me, I've seen it happen.

Maintaining Your Vision

Your vision – as in what you wanted for your fiction – must remain somewhere within the MS. Whilst editing, refer often back to your theme / moral / point, as we discussed earlier in this course. Make sure your editing is not destroying or undermining your vision. It's better to delete writing, even if it's good, that does not further your vision.

For instance, if you decided early on that you wanted to write a suspense novel and you have great swathes of text that do nothing to perpetuate that suspense, delete them.

Freshness

"Freshness" is a term bandied by publishers who probably have as little idea what they mean as we do. In reality they mean 'originality of voice' and, if you don't know what that means either, think of it as simply removing clichés and tired metaphors. Not just the phrases we take for granted but also some of the plot elements.

If you've read a lot of unpublished manuscripts, as I have, you'll have noticed that the same ideas, the same way of dealing with scenes, the same plot lines re-appear over and over. What publishers want to see is stories they weren't expecting to read – plot lines that surprise them – and a voice that seems unique. To me this is all down to characterization. If your characters are interesting enough, they will lead the story in interesting and hopefully unexpected places – which is something that you defined at the beginning of the novel writing process. Trying to put 'freshness' in after the MS is complete is nigh on impossible but what you can do is try to edit out clichés, tired metaphor and sections of predictable story line.

Continuity

One of the things you might come up against is problems remembering little things like the age and facial characteristics of your heroes.

In *Madame Bovary* for instance, the main character's eyes change color three times in the first fifty pages – but the author didn't have access to a computer when he wrote it so perhaps he's forgiven!

You might want to keep little cue cards listing various pertinent facts that you will need to refer to every now and then. Put all your notes together. I have maps of my fictional towns that I use to make sure characters have enough time to make journeys etc in the story.

Polishing

After about the twentieth pass – no, really, twenty is about right – over your MS, you'll be getting to feel that you cannot improve it any more. The text is smooth and crystal clear. Everything is beautifully presented, clean and error free.

This is what you need. This is the only kind of MS you want to send in to publishers.

As far as motivation is concerned at this point it's about staying clear. Your focus now is on the main goal – publication. Presentation is key. We'll look at all the dos and don'ts of submitting in the next module but for now be aware that it's only your best, your very best work that must go out. If you have any doubts about your MS – like that you wouldn't show it to someone else, or you're embarrassed about something in it, or you think there are errors that can be fixed later, then don't send it out.

This may mean reworking your MS from time to time until you feel it's ready. But that's what we must do. You should never be afraid to revisit your MS, continually, and make improvements.

Module Twelve

Getting Published

Mark Twain once said, "Anyone who says they don't write for publication is either a fool or a liar." If you take your writing seriously, of course you want to be read and respected for your efforts. What would be the point otherwise?

Also, if you didn't want to be widely read, why would you want to improve?

To believe you're writing for posterity is to kid yourself. When was the last time you heard of an author that 'rose from the dead' to critical acclaim? I can think of only one or two examples.

You see, it doesn't work that way.

In order for the next generation to fully appreciate your talent, you have to prove it to this generation. You have to prove you know what you're doing and can do it well. That's what this course has been about: proving to current publishers, editors, critics and reviewers that you're a good writer – and know what is required to entertain and enthrall the reading public.

That's why I've spent so much of my time during these modules showing you what is required. Of course there are many open ended debates amongst writers about the best and most effective ways to write and develop material – but there's very little debate out there amongst publishers, critics and the reading public. To them, it's simple, either you're a good writer – with interesting ideas well expressed – or you're not.

If you're still in any doubt as to the strength of your own material and its suitability for publication, it's most likely because you're still having trouble accepting the main principles of this course – that good fiction writing can be learned. And by simply following 'the rules' you can become a good, professional author.

So, before you send out your next manuscript, go back and re-read this course to see if you have followed its tenets – and repair your work, if necessary – before you show it to the world.

Now, we'll look at the specifics regarding getting published.

What Do You Really Want?

One of the key factors involved in getting published is deciding why you're doing it.

What do you want from publication?

It's not enough just to say fame and riches – that's too nebulous. I've spoken to many agents and publishers in the past that say the same thing: they want authors to have specific but realistic plans for themselves and their work.

Where do you see yourself in five years time? Ten years time? How many books will you want to have written? What kind of writer do you want to be? Is writing a bestseller a whim or a serious personal goal? Are you prepared to write four or five or six novels before your talent is recognized, by which I partly mean you're earning enough money? Or do think you won't last the race and will probably let life and disappointment get in your way?

These are important questions, especially in today's competitive writing market. To ensure success you will need to persist. You will need to improve. More importantly, you will need to WANT to improve, consistently. Bear in mind that according to the American Society of Authors, most 'professional' writers earn less than $12,000 a year from their writing – at first. It's only those that persist and hone their craft for the market that rise above this average figure to become   wealthy,   best   selling   writers.

Of course you have to love writing – or at least feel a compulsion that you can't control. But you also need to be businesslike about it. Are you really prepared to write for a few hours every day. Can you afford to do that? And for how long?

Finally, do you have the right attitude towards criticism and rejection? Do you see them as bad things – because they're not!

Publishers and agents are in truth desperate to see good manuscripts because most are pretty bad.

Successful writers will tell you they received comments and guidance on their work all through their lives. They've been encouraged, nurtured, yes, but also slammed and their writing hacked to pieces. Too often writers take criticism badly and go away and hide under a rock for years, forever sometimes, rather than admit their writing isn't wonderful.

Don't be like that.

Listen to criticism.

Absorb it.

Act on it.

And you will be rewarded.

Amazon & Kindle

Elsewhere I have written at length about self-publishing with Amazon and Kindle. Despite its growing popularity as an author solution, the majority of authors I teach are still very resistant to the idea that anything other than legacy publishing actually counts as success. Of course this idea is absurd. However, rather than lecture you about the future of publishing within these pages, I will present what most authors seem to want to know!

Feel free to look at my Amazon Author page if you'd like more information on writing for Amazon and Kindle - and actually making money from writing books..

Writing Queries

The hardest part of the submitting process to me is finding

appropriate markets. I'm not sure why but hunting through market listings gives me a headache – literally!

It always seems as though, despite there being thousands of publishers out there, it's difficult to find the right ones for your manuscript when it's ready.

The only way to get around the problem is to just do it. Study the market listings in Writers Market (US), Writers Marketplace (Australia) and Writers Guide (UK), look hard at their submission guidelines and see what kind of work they publish. Combine this with a search on the Internet and compile your own list of the publishers you think will look favorably on your writing.

Also be on the lookout for new publishers and agents too, whether by hunting bookshops, libraries or by reading industry publications. Always look for the most current contact name you can find – though I've discovered this is often a fruitless task, given the fast turnover of staff nowadays.

The cover letter for a fiction query should be as simple as possible. *Dear X, Please find enclosed my manuscript submission: XXX for your consideration. Yours, Author,* is actually enough. You can add more information if you like – there are actually no hard and fast rules, all authors are different, but never extend the cover letter on to a second page without a very good reason.

CV or not CV?

Here's a tip. If you have a long resume of publications, put them on a separate sheet with a brief bio and a picture of yourself if you've got one. If you don't have a long list of previous publications then put a brief bio of yourself in the cover letter – and I mean brief!

Contrary to logic, your impressive CV will not particularly help your submission – each author's work is usually based on merit. In fact, if you think about it, having a long list of published works means that you have more to live up to in your submission. Really what the publisher is looking for is to see whether you are the appropriate person to be submitting this kind of work. There's nothing wrong with saying, "This is my first novel. It is thriller based on my experiences as a police officer / social worker / administrative assistant or whatever." Remember that the vast majority of new writers do not / cannot write full time – so there's nothing wrong with admitting that.

Submission

Most fiction publishers want to see the first three chapters of your work along with a synopsis. If you write short chapters you might consider sending in the first 10000 to 15000 words – but be aware most publishers will know whether they like your work within the first 100 words, hence the necessity to work hard on your beginning.

Oprah once said that readers should ignore the first chapter of a modern novel because it was written to impress a publisher. She said the real author's voice generally doesn't come through until chapter two. Of course the publishing world howled and stamped its feet – protesting far too much – but I think she had a point!

The Synopsis

The word itself can send shivers of dread through even the most seasoned author. But having read thousands of them in my time, I can set your mind at rest. There is no real format or formula that works better or more effectively than any other – it depends on your personal style – as it should.

My preference is to tell the story, in the present tense, as though I were relating it to a friend. If you've done your job with the characterization and the plotting, you should have enough intrigue, conflict and drama in the story to make the synopsis sing, or at least hum a little.

One thing I've noticed over the years though is that the synopsis doesn't necessarily have to reflect the story very accurately. Making the synopsis work as a self contained story is more important than putting in everything that's in the novel. But just like screenplay outlines, the novel synopsis should contain the ending of the story. No ellipses or cliffhangers here, please.

But don't agonize over the synopsis too much. They should be light, engaging and easy to read but really their main function is to show that you can tell a story – and give the publisher a good excuse not to read it. I've witnessed publishers rejecting stories on their synopses, yes, but the fact is they were invariably going to reject them anyway – for reasons that had nothing to do with the authors or their writing. It's a fickle business.

Your Options

I'm going to assume at this point that your main goal is publication with trade publishers.

Of course, self publishing is an option – many successful writers have used it to their benefit – but for the purposes of this section, let's assume it's low on your priority list. That's understandable – if only in that you don't really know if your writing is any good if you self publish.

No amount of praise from POD houses, online vanity presses like Lulu or Publish America, offline printers, your family or friends will really convince you that your fiction writing is actually publishable in the mass market.

In a sense, only a real bona fide publishing deal with a reputable offline trade publisher is a true endorsement of your talent – and salability. Another good way to judge the commerciality of your work is to publish them as ebooks with Amazon, Kobo and iStore etc.

Though it's not written in stone, the best books tend to sell well on these sites - if you get everything right: well written MS, great cover and a good description etc.

But take comfort if you publish online and your work doesn't sell very well. The Net is not the best market for fiction – never has been – even for established authors.

There's something about a real book that simply can't be beat. And contrary to what the Net predicted a few years back, the sale of real paper books is actually rising.

Career Management

Many writers see getting their book published as the end result of their efforts. It's their main goal and they most times cannot see beyond it. This is a mistake. For serious writers, publication marks the beginning of an exciting new career.

Remember that success, especially in writing, is not an event or a specific place. It's not something you didn't have one day and miraculously appeared the next.

Writing success is a journey, a process, a series of events that can usually only be tracked through hindsight.

It's hard to imagine that Dan Brown was actually struggling after his first three novels. His publishing company was unimpressed by his lackluster sales and dropped him… until another publisher, going out on a limb, trusted that his next book, *The Da Vinci Code*, might just fare a little better. The rest, as they say…

JK Rowling was serially rejected (probably rightly so) by every major publisher until a tiny publishing house whose career was uncertain decided to try creating a Tolkeinesque niche for her amongst 10 year olds.

It's hard to grasp now but the fact is *Harry Potter's* hold on the imagination took around five or six years and three novels to surface… before exploding on to the scene when *Warner Brothers* bought the rights to her books.

It's all about persistence – and self belief.

Interestingly, both of the above writers do not impress the critics – so it's clearly not 'great writing' per se that guarantees success.

I think it's more to do with your vision as a writer, telling good stories well, and an unerring belief you're doing what is right, that is much more likely to get you there.

Read This Before You Start
Your Novel

As you will have gleaned from my *Easy Writing System* so far, writing fast and well is all about preparation.

It's vital that you are totally ready BEFORE you begin the great task ahead.

Therefore, before you start, I want you to go over the following 6-point checklist.

Ponder each point and follow instructions, where appropriate.

You might want to print this section out and go over it at your leisure. I believe it is critically important to your novel writing success.

1. Are you mentally prepared?

Hopefully you have been following some of the advice in the book about cleansing your mind and body of negative thinking and bad influences.

You should be feeling optimistic, energized and probably a little nervous too.

That's good.

You will need to remain healthy and focused during the days ahead. So, a couple of days before you start, do nothing, try to relax and unwind. You will need all your energy when it comes to writing your novel.

2. Have you allocated sufficient time?

Have you cleared the decks? Do the people around you know that you will be writing and cannot be disturbed? Even if you have only put aside an hour or two a day - can you be absolutely certain that time will not be impinged upon? I hope so.

It's vital you maintain continuity. For the next month, even when you're not writing, you will need to be totally 'in touch' with your novel and not lose your thread.

Commit yourself now to writing every day.

An aside: Many of my students find that towards the latter half of their novel they are writing almost continuously, and even dreaming of their book when they're asleep! You must be prepared for this - and have nothing, except your novel, planned for the next month.

3. Are your characters fully developed?

Before you start writing proper, you will need to ask yourself the above question.

You should know your major characters inside out - that way you won't have to stop writing to ask yourself how they will act and react in your story.

It should be natural and obvious to you (or at least your subconscious).

As a pointer, you will probably know when your characters are ready because they will seem like real people to you who can't wait to tell you their story!

If this is not happening, you might need to do some more work on them.

4. What is your theme?

This is the short phrase that sums up your novel - its point and purpose. For instance: 'Love conquers injustice.' Or 'The pursuit of money leads to death.'

Write out your theme now and print it out. Place it in your writing space. Tape it to the wall in front of you or stick it to the top of your computer screen.

Look at it often when you're writing. Never forget that everything that you write in your novel should be proving this theme. Use it to help you shape scenes and move chapters along.

ADVICE: Over the next few weeks, when family and friends ask you what you're writing about – as they inevitably will! - quote them your theme and nothing else.

You're not being cryptic, you're answering their question but keeping to a major tenet of the Easy Writing System. That is, 'Keep it to yourself!'

5. Do you have your story statement?

You will need to have your one or two-sentence story statement clear in your mind before you start writing.

It is more specific than the theme, as in, 'John gives up everything, his job, his house and almost his sanity in pursuit of his wife's killer.' Or 'They say good things come to those who wait. But when Sarah met Cliff, she wasn't going to wait forever.'

Though not as critical as your theme, it is important to let your subconscious know that you can describe your story succinctly. I am often amazed at how many writers start their novels without knowing what their story is about - a sure-fire recipe for disaster!

Don't fall in to this trap. Write out your story statement at the top of your template and read it once before every writing session.

6. Have a complete template

Your template is the whole of your story in note form.

Before you start writing, make sure that your template is complete, in sequence, you know your novel's ending and that there are no gaping holes you are planning to fill in when you get there.

A few minutes now spent working on plot gaps will save huge amounts of time and worry later.

Read over your story template several times, get the feel of your novel in your mind. Does it work? Does it have balance? Most importantly, does it prove your theme?

Okay? Lecture over!

When you've checked off the above points then, and only then, I believe are you ready to start writing for 30 days - or less, depending on how well you do!

So, get ready and go for it!

The very best of luck to you.

PART THREE

The Easy Way to Write

The 30 Day Formula

Day One

I'm assuming you'll get up early on Day One, and be at your PC or notebook by 6 am! I hope so. You'll need to put in about an hour's work now. That's right, just an hour…

Characters Characters Characters

First of all, you need characters – before anything else.

I remember a novice writer once asking me whether it was possible to have a novel without characters. I thought about it for a while. It was an intriguing idea.

You could write about scenery – but not for very long I would guess. You could write about plants or volcanoes or stars or any number of inanimate things. I'm not sure how interesting all this would seem to a fiction reader. Pretty soon you would need something more to keep the reader's interest.

Besides, even if the work is all description, isn't there a character implied? The reader is still conscious that the information is being transmitted to him or her via a human observer.

In that sense, it is therefore impossible to tell a story without at least one character – the writer!

The simple fact is, without characters there is no story. There is no point of view and no change to report on except the colors and patterns of nature. Without characters your novel would be a short work, I suspect.

Besides, readers want characters more than anything else. More than settings, drama, clever plots, thrills or gadgets. First and foremost, readers want people they can relate to. People they like or love, or hate. Without characters, there's no life to a story.

Some novices may be complaining now.

I have a story, a plot already. Can't we start there?

No. Never.

Your characters dictate the story. It should never happen the other way round.

Characters first – every time.

On Day One take a piece of paper and write out some ideas for characters. For instance:

*   *Girl, twenty-four, attractive, an anthropologist.*
*   *Man with a limp*
*   *Doctor, black, middle-aged, suave*

And so on.

You may already have ideas for characters. If so, develop them. Make them larger than life if you can. Modern fiction is about creating people we might like to be, rather than showing what we're really like.

Give them foibles, distinguishing features, unique ways that they do things, like:

*   *A stutter*
*   *A fear of heights*
*   *A medical condition*
*   *An odd religious persuasion*

If you don't have any ideas, think of people you know and the character traits you like or have impressed you. Do you know anyone adventurous, timid, gregarious, or shy?

What makes these characters intriguing? Is it a combination of things?

Probably.

Most interesting characters – especially in fiction – seem contradictory on the surface.

For example, you might have a highly moral character with a

weakness for brandy. Or a complete hedonist with a heart of gold.

Try not to think along your normal lines – keep pushing. Think: How far can I take this person? How complex can I make them? When do they stop being believable?

Remember: don't think of stories or plots at all at this stage - think only about characters.

All sorts of them: heroes, villains, businessmen, soldiers, accountants, mothers, sisters, fathers, brothers, friends, bad people, killers, dictators, and hated enemies.

Anything you like – have fun inventing people.

Do this for an hour or so until you have perhaps a half dozen you're happy with.

Only when the characters are beginning to take shape in your mind, should you give them names. Do this too early on and you might limit your imagination – you tend to think of people you already know with those names.

Names should help to make your characters come alive, in concrete form – so don't do it too soon. Make sure your characters deserve a name before you give them one!

If you have trouble thinking of names, look them up in the White Pages, or the Bible - anywhere. Pick a surname here and a Christian name there. Don't choose real names if you can help it – you never know who you might accidentally offend!

People who have the same name as your characters – especially famous people – are quite within their rights to sue you for damages if they think you have deliberately tried to defame them. Being oblivious to this fact is no defense in a court of law.

Next, think about their physical appearances, their particular distinguishing features.

Try not to think in terms of cliché. Make your characters real. Close your eyes and try to visualize them. Are they tall, thin, fat, good looking or ugly?

Some writers use pictures torn from magazines to help them visualize their characters.

Others prefer to use their imagination.

If it helps, write out potted CVs for your characters. Imagine what they might be good at – and what their failings are. What are their professions? Their hobbies? Their interests? Describe them in detail – a page of notes for each person.

What are their relationships like? How do they get on with friends, family and strangers? Where would they go on holiday? What food do they like? What clothes would they wear? What would their homes be like?

You can never know too much about your characters.

Go as far as giving them birthdays, favorite colors and lucky numbers.

You don't have to go over the top but the point is – at this stage - to make the characters completely believable to you. You probably won't use half the detail you're compiling now but it is important that it's there, in your mind.

Readers like to take it for granted that you know your characters well even when you don't describe all the details to them.

Most of all, you must give your characters:

* *Motivation*
* *Agendas*
* *Traits that aid or belay them*
* *Potential*

Motivation

You need to know what drives your characters. Are they ambitious? Were they scarred by an event in their childhood? Have they been hurt in love? Or are they simply driven to be heroic?

Agenda

Ideally, your characters will be at odds with each other at some stage. Ask yourself, what is it that my characters want? Are they looking for love, sex, revenge, power, money, or a quiet life? Their agendas may be complex, idealistic or self-defeating. It's up to you. But it is important that you think hard about this. It's what makes characters come alive.

Traits

Do your characters have traits that help them – or hinder them - in their agendas? For instance, does Cathy's fitness regime help her to escape a mugger? Is Tom's career path thwarted by his propensity for alcohol? Is the killer afraid of spiders?

Potential

Most of all, your characters should have the potential for change – either for great good or perhaps evil. Readers nowadays expect the characters to grow within the plot.

Ideally, readers should be able to see, or at least try to guess, where the characters might go given certain information, how they might change given certain events. It is up to you to signal that your characters are capable of much more. It's a promise you make to the reader that your novel will deliver.

At the beginning of a novel, you have to make known to the reader quickly that a character has something they need to do, or wants to do. This helps your reader to identify with a character in a few seconds, and can keep them hooked. But without sufficient motivation and an agenda, a character is usually not interesting enough for a reader – and they will put your book down.

So, think through this carefully. Your character's motivations must be strong yet believable, they must be instantly recognizable as real people, and their agendas should be powerful and intriguing.

Now, take a break from writing. Do something else. Go for a walk or do some housework. Maybe you need to get off to work now anyway.

As you go about your business, let your characters slowly solidify in your mind.

Think about them – as you might old friends, with affection. Imagine them acting and reacting to the things that make up their lives. Have fun. Let them live and breathe, laugh and cry. Watch them and get to know them well.

Later on in the day, when you're ready – and you'll know when – go for:

Interactions

Choose 2 to 6 of your characters and get them to interact.

Imagine conversations they might have. Would they argue? Would their agendas clash?

If one of your characters would completely destroy another's chances of fulfilling their own agenda, you're on the way to creating compelling fiction.

This exercise can be mental. You don't have to write things down if you don't need to.

However, you may want to. All well and good.

Little snatches of dialogue can be helpful – especially if they're dramatic and emotionally charged.

Dialogue is good at this stage because it's fast. With just a few words, you can get a feel very quickly for the relationships your characters will develop. Also, you get to know them even better. You get to know who is strong, and who is weak. Who is charming, and who is brash and insensitive.

Keep asking yourself questions. Things like:

* *What if John did that?*
* *How would Donna react?*
* *Why did her friend Elsie look embarrassed?*
* *Why didn't Doctor Monroe seem surprised?*
* *Was Detective Judith Ross suspicious?*

Even if you have no inkling of a story yet, ask this type of question. It will help you. And give you ideas to explore.

Put your characters through their paces. Team them up and make them do outrageous and absurd things.

* *What if Dick and Janet held up a bank?*
* *Could they do it – and get away with it?*
* *What if they joined the circus?*

Even if you think your story will have nothing to do with these things, ask the questions anyway! Keep asking.

* *How would Paul feel if Barry mugged him?*
* *How would Pete deal with being sent into space with Erin?*

Try to imagine your characters interacting with real people. Your friends perhaps or famous people now and from history. How do they act – are they shy, inspired, scared?

Imagine, or write down, their conversations.

By now, certain interactions might suggest lines of story.

Not plot at this stage, just ways in which your character might inter-react to create compelling situations.

How would it progress? Would it end badly or end well?

Imagine all the possible scenarios involving your favorite characters. Imagine you're collecting scenes for possible inclusion in a long running serial, or soap opera. Get to know all your characters in this way so that you always know how they will react with each other.

This process may take anything from an hour to the whole day, depending on your imagination, time and confidence level.

At the end of the day, before you go to sleep, review your notes for a few minutes. When you're ready, turn out the light and close your eyes.

Relax and tell yourself you'd really like to wake up with an idea for a story. Nothing overly complex – just an idea.

Then go to sleep.

Day Two

With a bit of luck – and perhaps the residue of a dream - you should wake up with the tiniest, twinkling germ of an idea.

It could be nothing, just a feeling, a vague certainty that a character must experience this or that. Trust it. Go with it. It's your all-powerful subconscious talking!

   * *Des must overcome his phobias to defeat his nemesis*
   * *Jessica falls in love with her brother's murderer.*

Anything is good as a starting point.

Free Association

Spend the day thinking through situations – and see how far you can push them. Make them dramatic and exciting.

As possible story lines suggest themselves to you, place your characters in different settings. A city, the country, South America, India, Australia, on Mars perhaps. See how the setting affects various scenarios that might occur to you.

Then try changing certain aspects of possible stories.

For example. If your story is about a fight between two brothers over their recently departed father's property, try to imagine all sorts of scenarios. Not just the one.

Imagine how a natural disaster might impinge on it, or some other seemingly unrelated event. Try to see the scenarios from every angle.

How would events appear to someone else? A wife of one of the brothers. The mailman, a journalist.

Then make it bigger. Add weight to the characters. Make them richer or poorer, more villainous or more moral. Raise the stakes. Make the brothers Kings or Captains of Industry, or make them small time hoods. See how far you can go with each of your ideas.

Try changing the historical perspective, too.

Do strange and silly things like turning the characters into animals.

Keep going with this kind of lateral thinking until you find your mind continuously returning to an idea you like the most.

Keep on asking questions, developing angles, until the ultimate idea has solidified in your mind, until you're absolutely sure your story could not be told in any other way.

It's important that you decide on Day Two that you will come up with a story. This kind of focus forces your mind to supply you with a story – and often a very good one.

Story

It's about now you might still be thinking about that plot of yours – the one you've been carrying around for years.

I'm not suggesting that you throw it away. I'm just saying that for now, you should hold it in reserve – for perhaps another book.

The trouble with plots is that characters don't like them – at least they don't like them if they didn't think of them!

Consequently, if you force a plot onto characters, it won't work. You'll end up stuck.

I promise you. The lifeblood of fiction is people. Real people that readers believe in.

It doesn't matter how smart and clever your plot is, if the people playing it out aren't convincing, readers will simply not want read your book. That's the truth of it.

When you write a novel – or any kind of fiction for that matter – you must start with the characters first.

You must let your characters define their own actions and interactions and let the plot grow naturally from there. It is one of the spooky things about writing that you can't force characters to play out a plot they're not comfortable in. Writers always talk about this and a novice may find it either amusing or strange. It assumes fictional characters have a life of their own. Well, let me tell you right now, they do. And if they're not happy, they'll be the first to let you know!

It happens like this: you're half way through a novel – approaching a plot point that is crucial to the story.

Bang! Suddenly you find your character won't play along. You write out the scene. It doesn't work. You try again. No matter what you do, your character's performance has become wooden and unconvincing. In truth, he's squirming with embarrassment as you try and squeeze him into a hole that's the wrong size for him.

It's at this point that you have to give up, or start again.

Your character is saying: "I'm sorry but I just wouldn't do that."

Then you have to go through to the agony of going back to another point in the novel and working forward to the plot point again – only to find the character is still sitting there stubbornly refusing to move. Honestly, you don't want to go down this road!

I would guess that all professional writers have been there at some point.

It's horrible!

Don't fall into the trap. Do it right the first time!

Now we're clear on that, let's go for it.

Drafting a Simple Plot

On the evening of the second day, take a large sheet of paper – preferably A3 -and write, "START" in the bottom left hand corner and "FINISH" in the top right.

Pick a character – your favorite – and write their name just up from "START."

Think about their motivations and their agenda.

For instance,

David Brockwith, 24, is an assistant buyer for a large toy manufacturing company. He's bored with his life and craves excitement. He's a gifted artist but has never found a way of making any money at it. He idolizes Paul Gauguin and wishes he had the courage to give up his job and follow his dream.

Julie Rand, 19, is a model. She's beautiful but doesn't particularly think she is. She was adopted when she was very young and is now desperate to find her real father. She has dreams where she believes she remembers him. She wants to know why he abandoned her. Her guardians intimated that her mother died in mysterious circumstances.

At a party of a mutual friend, the two are introduced. They hate each other on sight.

In this scenario, at the bottom left of the page, you might write,

David meets Julie.

Think about what might happen. They hate each other but you know they were made for each other. What would bring them together?

Later, David gets too drunk to drive and Julie reluctantly offers to drive him home. On the way, a truck overturns in front of them. They crash and narrowly escape death. They are taken to the hospital together.

Making your way up across the page, you might next write, *Crash.*

In the middle of the night, a mysterious man visits Julie while she's asleep. David is awake – he'd gone to find her. He sees the man but is too shy to speak to him. When he's gone, from memory, David draws a picture. In the morning, he shows it to Julie.

"It's him," she cries out. "It's my father!"

The next thing you might write is,

David draws man, Julie recognizes father.

You get the idea. Keep working your way up to the top right hand corner, if at all possible, intensifying the action as you go. Set as many obstacles as you can in front of your protagonists efforts.

At this stage, don't be afraid to make mistakes. This is a rough draft of your story.

You're making it up as you go along, so don't worry.

If you get stuck, start again or scribble out bits that don't work.

If you start running out of paper, consider taking out earlier scenes that don't progress the action.

If need be, draw in subplots that might not be important but which appeal to you. But keep the action focused towards the goal – the

FINISH, whatever that might be.

You don't need to write out everything. At this stage, the barest skeleton of the plot is sufficient. You can flesh things out later.

Types of Plot

The most common type of plot is linear – that is, it's sequential.

This is the one I would recommend for the novice.

The reason for this is logic – it's the way the mind works, the way the brain likes to be told stories. One sequence follows another in a logical time frame, where each action is dependent or resulting from the last. It's most satisfying when the outcome of the story is loaded with meaning or revelatory in some way. Either way, the reader has to feel there was some point in being told the story – as I explained in the earlier modules.

Most stories are told in this linear fashion. Stories that require flashbacks are rare – and should be used with caution. Readers generally hate it when a flashback is used to justify a plot point that has been deliberately withheld. It can come across as a cheap trick – or a stroke of brilliance, depending on the skill of the writer!

There are numerous other types of plot. For the purposes of your 30-day novel however, I would stick with something relatively simple.

Telling stories from multiple points of view where actions and time overlap can be very confusing to write, let alone read.

Besides, people are so used to TV and movies now, they expect stories to be told in a certain way – that is, sequentially -and will often regard any other way as obscure.

There are various story types. Here are a few:

* The Learning experience
* The Moral
* The Quest
* The Comeuppance
* The Consequences of good/ evil actions
* Turmoil and Resolution
* Action / adventure
* Literary Meandering
* Genre: Romance / Mystery / Thriller / Suspense

It will be up to you to decide which type of story you are telling.

Sometimes you might not be able to easily categorize yours. That's okay.

Genres

There are also various genres, all of which have their own rules. A detailed look at each is beyond the scope of this book (but many of my genre specific titles are now available on Amazon - with more to come!) Here's a quick overview of the genres you might choose from (even though I'm convinced genres actually pick authors).
* *Romance*
* *Horror*
* *Science Fiction*
* *Fantasy*
* *Supernatural*
* *Crime*
* *Thriller*
* *Erotica*
* *Mystery*
* *Medical*
* *Action*
* *Adventure*
* *Military*
* *Historical*
* *Literary*
* *Mainstream*
* *Sagas*
* *Children's*
* *Young Adult*

Of course there are various sub genres and now, what is becoming increasingly popular, cross-genre (with writers), where one or more elements of a genre overlap into another.

The type of novel you write will probably reflect the type of novel that you read. Most writers read voraciously and tend to gravitate towards certain genres. Look at your book collection. See if there's a dominant type of novel there.

There is? My advice is go with that. It'll be something you understand and are comfortable with.

If you're not sure, think about what TV shows you like. Do you like mystery, doctor shows or soaps? Maybe you like Science Fiction. Whatever. Go where you feel you know the ground.

All of the above was about making choices. Final choices before the big one:

When should I start my novel?

Soon, soon, but not until you've read the rest of this section!

Defining your Goals

While the plot is still fresh in your mind, it's important to write down a few goal statements that you can keep beside you while you're writing.

This is crucially important to your novel. Without a few guiding principles, your story may go off track. It's important you keep it focused – and that you stick to your intentions.

Admittedly, this is something that most novice writers, and even a few professionals don't bother with. Some writers say they write better when they just make it up as they go along.

Whilst the technique might be good for certain individuals – like Stephen King, I think most of us would go off the rails very quickly without some kind of plan.

I've known many writers that complain that they start out okay – get about a third of the way into their novel and then have to stop because they realize they don't know what their story is about!

So, first things first.

It's much easier to write a novel if you have asked yourself these three simple questions before you start.

1. What's my book about?

2. What's the overriding theme?

3. What does the story prove?

Write out the answers to these questions. Try to keep them short. Pin them up over your writing area so that you are reminded of them throughout the book writing process.

In answer to the first question you might write,

Donnie must escape her evil husband to save her daughter's life.

In answer to the second question, you might say your book is about love defeating evil. The book proves there is hope in the world. Is the point worthwhile? On balance, probably yes, though it's been made a million times. Is there anything you can do to put a new angle, or shed new light on this old chestnut?

Believe me, it's very important to ask yourself these questions now. If you don't, they will come back to haunt you – especially if and when you're having a block.

The biggest single reason writers give up on their books is that they've lost sight of their original vision. After 50,000 words, telling the story doesn't seem so important anymore. So, they stop and agonize – often for months or years. Most times, they stop, disillusioned with their work and with writing itself.

You must not let this happen to you!

It is imperative that you have your vision set in stone before you write the first word! Therefore, ask yourself the questions above and write down your answers - read them and be sure that they have weight, substance and credibility.

Now – write a one-sentence synopsis of your story. For instance:

Jack sets out on a quest to find his wife's killer and discovers, to his horror, that it was his father.

You can make your sentence longer if needs be, but keep to the "one-sentence" rule. It will help you to focus.

Also, write down the central idea in one or two sentences. No more than a paragraph.

Like this:

Man kills wife out of jealousy - and lives to regret it.

Power corrupts the businessman - but he learns to love again.

Girl wants to find herself - and seeks revenge for being savagely beaten.

Think about your plot in relation to these statements.

Remember that everything in your story must be character driven. No events must transpire that are out of character.

If they are - no matter how interesting or quirky, you must abandon them - or go back to stage one – because you haven't fully finished your character analyses.

Whatever you do, don't plough on regardless and think things will work themselves out - they won't. They'll get worse as the plot becomes all the more complex.

Too many writers make this fundamental error.

I repeat: Don't start writing until you know what your novel is about!

Decisions, Decisions

It's about now you'll be coming to grips with how you are going to tell your story.

From one person's point of view? That is, following the hero? From multiple points of view? Where action and drama can occur outside of the hero's knowledge? But where the reader is always involved?

Perhaps your story will be told in the first person, where the "I" character isn't aware of action he doesn't directly experience.

There are many schools of thought here. It's assumed by some that novices find first person stories easier to tell. I'm not sure that's true. It can be limiting to have only one viewpoint, especially if the plot is complex. However, it can be entertaining for the reader – especially if your main character is interesting and fun. Problems arise when there's critical information to be relayed and the protagonist is not in a position to hear of it.

Multiple viewpoints are common because that's how TV and movies tell stories.

Readers are comfortable with this type of storytelling, especially when the majority of the action in centered around one "heroic" character.

The decision is finally yours but remember – you have to stick with it! If you don't, you might end up having to start the book again!

Where is the Story Set?

You will also about this time be getting a good idea where you are going to set your story.

It's a good idea to have this clear in your mind. It's also a good idea to know the places you'll be writing about.

Readers are very astute. They want authors to get the details right. If they can tell you've never been to the place you're describing – and the tiniest of details missed can give you away – you've lost them.

Make notes about your likely locations. If necessary, draw maps so you know how to get around. Think about the little details. What's the weather like at certain times of the year? What time does the sun go down in midsummer? How much traffic is there at any one time? What kind of wildlife is there?

Check out any of the buildings, offices and houses where you're going to place your actions. Don't guess what the inside looks like. Have a look.

The details are important – even if you don't describe them. Things that don't seem to matter while you're writing have a nasty habit of biting you back later!

Of course, if you're writing fantasy or science fiction, you have free rein to describe what you like. But here too, you must be consistent and believable.

Now is the time for some jealously guarded secrets…

The Six Killer Rules for Creating Fiction

Later we'll talk about how to create compelling fiction on every page of your novel.

For now, I want to give you an overview of what makes good fiction work.

If you want to write a brilliant novel, you must have these ingredients:

* *Involving, sympathetic characters right from the start*
* *Tense and dramatic situations*
* *Resourceful characters that have an agenda at odds with their circumstance*
* *Obstacles to the characters' success*
* *Drama and conflict that intensifies*
* *A final dénouement and/or a satisfying close*

It might be an idea for you to print off these instructions and place then in your writing area. If you always bear them in mind, you won't go far wrong in your fiction.

Day Three

Up nice and early today?

Good. It's time to start. You'll need some kind of outline now. So, it's time to introduce you to…

Designing a Template – or the 10 Step Plot Trick

When you're sure your story will work, you're ready to start.

I've deliberately left the most creative part – that is, coming up with the story – to you.

I think it's essential that the story come from you, unaided!

Take a sheet of A4 and write the numbers 1 to 10 down the left hand side. If you're using a computer so much the better – this sheet will become the template for your novel.

Next to Number 1, write what happens at the beginning, copying it from your plot diagram.

At Number 10, write down what happens at the end.

For example,

1. Mark discovers his wife, June, has been murdered.

2.

3.

4.

5.

6.

7.

8.

9.

10. Mark and Sally defeat the bad guy

Then go back and fill in the critical plot points that move your story forward.

1. Mark discovers his wife, June, has been murdered.

2. Police try to arrest Mark, he escapes.

3. Mark meets Sally.

4. They pursue mystery killer.

5. They unravel chain of evidence.

6. Sally kidnapped.

7. Mark finds her – nearly dead.

8. Killer revealed – it's a cop.

9. Car chase through Manhattan.

10. Mark and Sally defeat the bad guy.

Use short phrases - no more. Just enough so that you know what's happening. Key triggers you will use to keep you on track. This is also a very good way of seeing if your story actually works. If you can break down a story to its critical elements, and it still makes sense, you're probably on to a winner.

Actually, ten points is just a starting place. You may end up with 12 critical steps or 20 or 30, or maybe only 3 or 4. But you get the idea.

You might want to expand the whole process and draw diagrams and flowcharts and the like, but I wouldn't. Keep it simple.

I know lots of writers do those relational bubble graphs – where they brainstorm all the connections and relationships between the characters and their actions. To me there is a very good reason for not doing them.

They confuse the mind.

Telling a story is sequential. It moves from one point to the other like the words that flow one after the other in a sentence.

Your writing progresses in a linear way, one word after the next, one sentence at a time.

Surely that's how you should make sense of your ideas.

A sheet of jumbled circles, crisscrossing lines and text does nothing to help you actually write you novel. It just proves you have a complex idea.

The trick, every time, is to simplify. That way – you're always going to be in control.

Keep events and plot points in the right order, get the story to make sense sequentially.

If you don't like it, or it's not working, simply start again.

Filling In The Gaps

Take your template and start making quick notes in between the critical plot points, using your diagram if you need to. Write notes that link the key events. Use short phrases again that will trigger your intentions when you write. Don't overdo it. You are merely building a framework on which to hang your novel.

By the end of this process, you should have about 2 or 3 pages of a plot outline.

You can pin this up or save it as a file. Also, rename it and keep it separate. It will come in handy later on when you need to write a synopsis of your novel.

But use the file as the actual template for the book. That way, whenever you're wondering where the story should go next – you have it already on your screen, usually just under where you're writing.

This can be enormously comforting when you're writing – knowing that the book is, in effect, written. All that you're doing is filling in the gaps.

Ready, Steady...

The fact is, if you've done everything I've suggested up until now, the novel is merely a formality. In a sense, you've done the hard work. You have everything you need: characters, scenes, a plot, a theme and a point to prove.

Bravo. From here on in, it's all fun! So stop worrying and start enjoying being a writer!

The Opening Gambit

Early on at the start of your novel, you'll need to establish mood, setting and context.

Traditionally, it's what writers have been doing for centuries. However, things are different now. Readers are more sophisticated than they used to be and consequently get bored of too much description.

They like to know what's going on immediately, and who it's happening to. More importantly, you have to make the reader care.

It is therefore critical that your readers like your characters.

Creating involving and sympathetic characters that grab your readers' attention from the first page is probably easier than you think. It's a case of what you focus on when you first introduce them.

When you start writing, try this:

Get Them On Your S.I.D.E.

S.I.D.E. is an acronym for Sympathy, Identification, Drama and Empathy. It's a simple way to remember the golden rules for introducing characters.

Almost from the first sentence you must try to evoke sympathy for your character.

Place them in a position that the reader can relate to immediately.

Consider the following opening lines:

Jane pulled her collar up against the pounding rain.

Jack heard the news of his father's death but couldn't believe it.

She pulled the car to a halt, sobbing.

He hated dentists; this one especially.

Next, you need more than pure sympathy. You want to make the reader think,

Yes, that's how I would react. That's like me. I would do that.

In short, you'll want your reader to quickly identify with the character.

To do this you'll need to introduce a common, universal emotion or activity, most likely in the next couple of lines. Something like,

Jane knew she shouldn't be out in the rain. Her mother would have a fit.

Jack tried to focus on his father's face, but the memory proved elusive.

The woman looked in the rear-view mirror, wiping mascara from her cheek.

The drill felt large in his mouth – too large.

See what I mean? The reader has been forced into the middle of the action. He has a ringside seat, as it were. Now you need to involve the reader in some drama, before he or she loses interest and gets bored!

In this context, drama can be defined as the character interacting with their environment. The reader doesn't want your characters to be passive. The reader wants them to take action.

For instance,

It was no use, Jane decided. She was going to have to look for him. She stomped along the wet street in the direction of the school.

Jack pounded the table and picked up the phone to call Annie.

Satisfied she looked better - a little better anyway - the woman drove on.

Suddenly, the man grabbed the dentist around the throat. He began to squeeze.

In the case of the last line, we are clearly dealing with an unsympathetic character, perhaps a killer. That's okay. You've tricked your reader into having sympathy and identifying with him, perhaps to shock.

This is okay once in a while. However, most readers want heroes. Writing about antiheroes can make your work doubly hard to consume for one simple reason. If your reader doesn't like your characters, they won't care what happens to them.

Which brings us to the final element of S.I.D.E.

Empathy

Within a short space of time, you want your reader to feel they are completely in tune with your hero, and are rooting for him or her. To do this, add a little something to your character that will warm the reader's heart. Or at least something that makes your character seem deeply human and likable.

For instance,

Jane looked up at the tall rain-spattered building. Her son was in there somewhere. The son she would gladly die for.

He heard Annie's voice. The tears came then, so fast he couldn't speak.

She drove into her hometown, back to sanity, back to the places she loved.

The man quickly released his grip. It was happening again. He needed help – badly.

Okay, this kind of formulaic writing might seem like a cheap trick to you. But the fact is, it works. Especially if you don't make it obvious.

Didn't you feel yourself being drawn in with just a few words? Your chief job is to force the reader read on. And to do that nowadays you need to use every trick in the book!

This book!

Before you go to bed tonight, think how you are going to open your novel the biggest and best way you can. It's important. Some readers – especially agents and publishers - will only ever read your opening paragraph!

Day Four

Hopefully you've negotiated with your family and friends and loved ones and managed to set aside an hour or two for your writing - every day for at least the next 25 days.

If so, you're ready to roll.

Just before you leave the starting blocks, I want to teach you something else that is guaranteed to turn an average novel into a brilliant novel – every time!

Writing – Q.E.D.

Q.E.D. is another little acronym to help you remember what you need for creating compelling fiction on every page of your novel. Q.E.D. stands for:

Question
Empathy
Drama

Questions encourage people to look for answers. When readers read fiction they are asking themselves a series of questions about your characters and about your story.

Their own Commentator is kept busy dealing with your character's problems rather than their own – which is why reading is still so popular, by the way.

Only when you satisfy your reader by feeding questions and later on providing answers will the reader feel entertained.

At the beginning of a new sheet of paper, ask yourself,

What question am I going to place in the reader's mind on this page?

You must have one – it's what makes the reader keep reading. Without constantly stoking curiosity, a reader will simply get bored and not read on.

Empathy is crucial too. We looked at this. Not only is it important that you create empathy for your characters early on, you will also need to keep reinforcing it as you go.

Hopefully the actions that your characters make will take care of some of this. But you should be aware that if you feel your characters slipping away from you, it's probably because you're not keeping them human enough to be compelling.

A reader's total empathy with a character can be powerful. It is the hallmark of all good fiction writers. To create a hero that is credible and popular is the goal of most leading authors. Because once you've done that, you can take your readers almost anywhere.

When it's done well, the reader is totally in the your thrall and will trust you to take him further, on the adventure that is your novel, or series of novels.

Use it consciously. Readers rarely spot that you're doing it deliberately. They only know what they like and that is, for the time they are reading, they like being your lead character.

Lastly, D is for Drama again. It's important that you create drama, conflict and tension at least once on every page. It's the way of modern fiction.

People want to be entertained. But they've seen it all before. On TV and at the movies.

You don't need long explanations or descriptions of things they are familiar with. It's just not necessary.

Readers want to be thrown into the thick of things immediately. There are a hundred ways to do that but most of them involve action, conflict and drama. If you find yourself wandering from the point and nothing in particular is happening, cut back to where the last piece of conflict was, delete all the verbiage and static writing and move off again – this time at high speed!

Imagine you're a soap opera writer where every scene counts, and every exchange is emotionally charged. Try not to sink into melodrama – but be aware that you're writing primarily to entertain.

At the beginning and ending of every new page ask yourself:

Q.E.D? Have I fulfilled the three requirements of compelling fiction?

If the answer is yes then you're on the way to becoming the next bestseller writer!

Setting: The Other Character

Novice writers tend to forget that setting can not only enhance your writing but also give it depth and a whole personality of its own. In most novels, the action is just as important as where its taking place. Try to think of setting as "the other character" when you're writing your scenes. This helps you to focus on it and give it adequate treatment.

You don't need to say much. It's surprising how much readers pick up from just a couple of well placed words and phrases.

It is also a useful tool for mood enhancement. Try not to be heavy handed with the symbolism. Lightning cracks at critical moments.

Sunshine at the end of a book. That sort of thing. They're clichés.

No mention at all of scenery and surroundings is usually not enough. Always remember to say something about the setting. If nothing else, it's a useful way of breaking up dialogue!

Day Five

When you're writing, monitor your word count. Keep a record of it.

Set targets. Get to know what you can expect of yourself and remember to write fast!

That way you get to stop quicker when you've reached your goal.

Don't beat yourself up if you don't make the targets. Some days you'll do better than others. Some days you might not write at all. Just stay focused and don't lose sight of the fact you must return to your writing desk – as soon as you are able. Long gaps, as in more than 24 hours, between writing stints are definitely to be avoided.

Day Six

Automatic writing

I believe the term "Stream of Consciousness Writing" was first coined by Hunter S Thompson, the famous gonzo journalist.

He too, discovered that writing quickly - basically without thinking - was the best and easiest way to write a lot quickly. He developed this technique on the political campaign trails he used to report on.

He didn't have time to take proper notes or even have a proper desk to write from. He wrote on campaign buses and in hotel rooms.

The interesting thing about his reports is that they are extraordinarily detailed. You really get a feel for what it must have been like following around these obsessed politicians as they wheel and deal their way around the country.

The other remarkable aspect of Thompson's work is that, despite the apparent speed with which it was written, it's quite literary. It gives a lie to the idea that writing fast is tantamount to writing badly. It seems as though actually the opposite is true.

The good news then is, if you trust your subconscious and you don't concentrate too hard – letting the words and ideas flow – the writing is better!

Perhaps it should be more accurately called stream of subconscious-ness, because it requires no more effort that you sitting down and typing. No need for worry, talent or inspiration. Switch off and plug into your back-brain.

It knows best.

So keep going. Don't look back at anything.

Write and write without thinking about the writing. Think only about the story and where it's going. Let your mind wander. Try not to think of the mechanics of getting the words out. At this stage spelling mistakes or slips of the fingers don't matter.

Keep going. It gets easier with practice.

Day Seven to Day Ten

Technique

Writing is 1% inspiration, and 99% perspiration.

You've heard that one of course. I prefer to think that writing is actually 99% technique – and that it can be learned and taught.

Look at the great artists in history. Homer, Leonardo, Michelangelo, Shakespeare. They studied their craft. They knew it so well; they knew how to bend it like putty, to make it work in their hands. There is no mystery involved here, no special powers.

Fortunately, in modern fiction writing there are some very simple rules. I've tried to include as many as I can in this book, so that you'll never need to go anywhere else.

What follows is a list of fundamental mistakes that writers make. If you avoid these traps, there's no reason why you shouldn't create highly acceptable fiction.

The Ten Deadly Writing Sins

1. Self indulgence – flowery language, lack of focus.
  2. Author's voice – intruding in to the text, making value judgments.
  3. Telling – has its place but showing is better.

4. Lack of place – where the setting is indistinct. Place is the other character!
5. POV switches – results in reader confusion.
6. Cliché – when you can't be bothered to think of something better.
7. Unsympathetic characters – publishers' frequent complaint.
8. Woolly plotting – where nothing advances the story.
9. Cheap tricks – like withholding crucial information.
10. Lack of love for your characters. If you don't, who will?

Keep these rules in mind as you write.

And don't forget to write fast.

Have fun too. Make your scenes big and memorable. Come in with a bang and go out with a metaphorical dotted line. Be dramatic, provocative, witty, clever, but most of all, make the drama and conflict sparkle.

Like the best sex – do it with love and you'll do it well.

Day Eleven to Day Fourteen

You're sat at your desk, ready to go. You know that if you keep on writing 3000 to 5000 words a day, you'll have your novel finished in less than a couple of weeks now.

Easy.

So…

Why don't you feel like writing?

There could be lots of reasons.

Probably the one that's uppermost in your mind is the sheer enormity of the task in front of you. You've written a lot and it seems as though you have so much more to do!

Take heart.

Everything is possible if you break it down into small enough pieces. Don't aim too high. If you're having trouble with a large complex section, cut and paste small pieces of it to other blank documents.

Try not to think of the whole thing. Just the next line, the next paragraph, the next interaction or the end of the current chapter.

Small successes will eventually drive you on to the larger goal.

Fear will end in failure and misery. Don't take on too much in one go. Relax and enjoy it.

Remember the golden rule: Don't think. Write.

Day Fifteen to Day Nineteen

Here's a useful tip.

Before you start a writing session, do this simple meditation exercise. It works wonders.

Close your eyes, relax and breathe deeply three times. Then say to yourself:

With every word I write I become more calm, confident and creative.

Say it three times, with feeling. Imagine you are typing or writing quickly, fluidly, smiling to yourself with the simple pleasure of it all.

Trust your subconscious. Tell yourself you won't question the wisdom of the subconscious. That you won't question what you write - yet. Let go.

When you open your eyes you'll simply walk to the PC or your notebook and just write – without even thinking.

Day Twenty to Day Twenty Three

Remember to keep your mind and body healthy.

When you're not writing go for pleasant walks or trips to relaxing places – like art galleries and libraries.

Don't expect you'll be able to go out with your mates on a Friday night and you'll be fine to write in the morning. It doesn't work that way. You need to be clear and fresh when you write – so pick appropriate times.

Keep pushing, though. Don't lose sight of the goal. You're almost there now – just a few more days to go!

Don't think. Write.

Day Twenty Four

Okay, if you're really struggling with your output at this stage, don't despair. You have a couple of alternatives, both of which are valid.

Some writers at this point will put in some extra work. They'll know they're capable of finishing the task but that they will need more time actually writing.

Fair enough. Perhaps renegotiate with those around you and put in twice the writing time over a weekend. Four to six hours on a Saturday and Sunday could boost your output to 25,000 to 40,000 words in one fell swoop. If you do this, take a break of ten minutes every hour – mainly to keep your body from complaining too much.

The other alternative, if you really don't think you can achieve the requisite word count, then by all means take a break. Perhaps a couple of days, or a week. To recharge your batteries or get your head clear again. Imagine the 30 day clock is frozen and you will start it again the next time you come back to write.

Don't take too long though. You don't want to lose the momentum you've generated.

Day Twenty Five

Phew!

All being well, you should have finished or nearly finished your first draft. If not, come back to this section when you have.

Take a day off to relax. You deserve it.

Now, there's a school of thought that says you should put your first draft away for a few weeks or months to get some distance from it. I'm never sure this is good advice, at least for the very first pass.

I've known many writers who've done this and never come back to their manuscripts.

If they do, they're so far away from it, they don't know where to start!

If you're the sort of person who can't bear to edit their work without putting it aside for a while, then do just that. Come back to the following section when you feel you're ready.

For everyone else my advice is, while it's still fresh, go back through your manuscript and at least repair the nuts and bolts – now!

Don't work too hard at this. Don't sweat it. Relax. Go on autopilot.

Check the little things like spelling. Put in missing words. Delete the odd glitch. Don't, I repeat don't, make any substantial changes yet. Your writing is better than you think.

Now, I'm Going to Tell You Something Very Important

A little known secret that will blow you away.

When people read your book, they aren't actually reading your book.

Huh?

That's right. People aren't actually reading your book. No. They're reading their own book. The one that's in their head - as they read yours!

This is good news. Excellent news, in fact. Let me explain.

The way it works is this...

There is a tacit understanding between a writer and a reader that is based on trust.

The reader has to let go when he or she reads fiction. Some call it willing suspension of disbelief, or the fictive dream. Others call it hypnotism.

That's why writing is popular. It fulfils a purpose – and the purpose is to transport the reader to another world! This can only be done with trust. And it is part of the writer's "trust contract" with the reader not to break the spell.

As long as you follow the basic rules of fiction writing and make sure your writing flows with an easy, uncomplicated rhythm, the reader will feel compelled to continue.

Because once the reader's in that semi-hypnotized state, the reader's mind wanders. It has to. It's how it conjures up the images you are placing in their mind. In a sense, their minds are literally melding with yours – over distance - creating a reality that is not quite yours but something more akin to their interpretation of your novel.

If you speak to professional writers they will tell you that they often receive letters from fans thanking them for writing a book they didn't know they'd written!

That's because your book is essentially different for everyone that reads it. It's unique in that sense because each person is unique and will take in the information and story presented in their own unique way.

That's why I believe that writing quickly – from the subconscious – produces an infinitely more readable novel. Because it uses the same brain frequencies that the reader will use. I believe writing that is painstakingly overworked by continuous editing actually hampers this process. Editing might make a book more literary but it doesn't always make it easier to read.

To prove this phenomenon to yourself, pick up any best selling author's book.

Open up a page at random in the middle.

You'll immediately find there's something wrong. Sentences don't make sense. There seems to be words missing. Descriptions seem inadequate. Action appears disjointed.

There's a reason for this.

Back at the start of the book, the reader has already made a pact with the author. In the first few pages, the reader has adjusted to the writer's style. He is trusting. He no longer needs all the obvious words and phrases to get what the author means.

That's why you shouldn't over-edit your book. Trust that your subconscious knew best.

You have something much more readable than you might think.

Day Twenty Six

F.A.S.T. Editing

Yep, it's another one of those snappy acronyms to help you remember how to edit – quickly and easily.

F.A.S.T. stands for: Flow, Appropriateness, Sense and Trust.

Flow

It's important that there's an innate rhythm to the writing. This can be more important than anything else at this stage because it's part of the hypnotic element you want to keep in your work.

Most writers find that after the first few pages, they stop editing so much. This is not always because the writing has gotten better. It's because the writer has got into his own hypnotic rhythm and has stopped being so fussy about his own words.

That is, he knows what he wants to say. It's there. It might not be perfect but the words do the job of conjuring up the right images at the right time.

Go through your manuscript mindful of clunky phrasing, wordiness, and over description. Take out anything that upsets the rhythm and makes you falter or frown while you're reading. Clean up sentences that are clumsy.

Appropriateness

This is also to do with trust, and the pact between the writer and the reader.

Nothing must jar. Make sure there are no sudden changes in point of view. Take out anything that might smack of authorial intrusion. If a character suddenly says something odd – if it's not essential - take it out.

Sense

Everything in your novel should make sense. If it doesn't, the reader will be thrown out of the spell.

Usually things don't make sense because the thought process is missing or you've skipped ahead of the action without any explanation, or perhaps missed a dialogue tag.

Sometimes this can mean simply inserting a sentence or two between points to ease the transition from one idea to another.

Other times, you'll find that, rather than spend a long time working on a particular idea or section; you might as well get rid of it.

Don't keep trying to rework prose if it's too hard!

Remember the old adage: "If anything strikes you as particularly fine writing, cut it out."

"Fine writing" is what readers skip nowadays. They're not interested. They just want the story.

And as Fitzgerald said, "Have the courage to kill your darlings."

Trust

If you're not convinced by a piece of action or drama, your reader won't be either.

Don't ever think that the reader is in any way inferior to you. Write with respect for your readers. Never insult their intelligence by leaving in something you think is "okay."

It is not okay at all. Write from the heart, with love and care about what you have written. The reader will respond accordingly.

Day Twenty Eight

You've probably spent the last two or three days going over the book, tightening everything up.

You've probably also woken up in the middle of the night and realized that buried deep with the text, or even the subtext, there are a few...

Logic Flaws

These usually fall into the following categories:
* *Events out of sequence*
* *Players acting out of character*
* *Impossible phenomena / circumstance*
* *Lack of sufficient explanation*

Most times these can be fixed by simple deletions of passages or just a few words added to paragraphs by way of exposition.

Sometimes there might massive holes in the very fabric of your story.

Do not despair. Before you launch in to do a botch repair job, show the story to a few objective outsiders. See if they notice first. Sometimes a writer's perception of his own work is faulty. Sometimes, if the writer points out the flaw in his work, the reader will say, "Well, yeah I know, but that's all part of the story, isn't it?"

Writers have a habit of over-explaining, especially if the idea or concept is unfamiliar.

The best piece of advice here is also an old adage.

Never justify or explain.

That's up to the critics, not you.

As long as your novel is consistent, the reader will pick up on the rest – and a lot more besides.

Day Twenty Nine

Go for one final speed-read.

Don't dwell on the prose. Get the sense of the story, how it ebbs and flows.

This is the way critics read. They have to – to get the review done before anyone else!

What do you think? Is it brilliant? I bet you think it is!

Day Thirty

OK? Finished? Printed off the book or have it as an email attachment?

Send it to some people you are not related to – maybe 3 or 4 that you know will read it rather than people who might not.

In a few days, ask them what they think. If there is agreement amongst them, fix the things they suggest. Leave well alone the things they like.

If they all say different things, don't worry about it.

If only one person violently objects to it, ignore them. Unless they're a respectable agent or an experienced editor, of course.

The fact is, there will always be someone who won't like your novel. But remember, this is true for best sellers too. You can't please everybody, so don't even try. At the end of the day, the only person's opinion that really matters is your own.

And Finally

You did it. If you've read this far, I am sure you are a person who can write novels. You know you are capable of doing the one thing most people dream about all their lives without taking action.

Congratulations!

Now, find out the addresses of all the appropriate agents and publishers you can find, and go out and post the thing! Who knows – your novel may turn out to be the next best seller!

By the way, if you read this book in one sitting, well done. Now go back and read it again. This time, do all the things you were told!

BONUS APPENDIX

A Proven Strategy for Getting Your Novel Taken Seriously by Agents and Publishers

Introduction

This guide is intended to help you on your quest for publication. It is based on the latest information gleaned from numerous writers, agents and publishing professionals. It is however, an entirely personal view.

The publishing industry offers no guarantees. Even successful authors sometimes have to go through the following process after they've had a 'hit' book, or even a series of 'hit' books. That's the reality of choosing a career in the Arts. You're only as good as your last – or next – success.

According to a recent Jenkins survey, there are currently around six million unpublished manuscripts in the US alone. Of course, only a fraction of these will ever see the light of a publisher's desk but still, you can see immediately that you are up against a steep uphill climb.

However, books currently sell well. The fact is about that one in fifty submitted manuscripts in the US do get published, and that many people in the industry do make money – a lot of money.

So don't despair. If you keep at it, one day it will be your turn.

For now the reality is that, as soon as you start submitting your manuscript, you will inevitably receive rejections. The important thing is not to take them personally – they rarely have anything to do with your writing.

John Grisham, Stephen King, Anne Rice and Patricia Cornwell collectively had their novels rejected hundreds of times before they were taken seriously. There's no shame in rejection – it's par for the course. Getting published is about persistence.

Think of it this way. Each rejection is actually one step closer to a sale. Hang in there and one day it will happen!

Plus of course many new authors are choosing to circumvent the system altogether and self publish their own work through websites like Amazon, Kobo and iStore. If you write well - and intend to write a series of novels in the same genre, this can be a very effective career path. For single novels however, you might still want to consider traditional publishers.

Tools

Firstly, you will need a current list of agents and publishers. In the US the most comprehensive guide is Writer's Market, published by Writer's Digest.

In the UK, it's the Writer's and Artist's Yearbook published by A & C Black.

In Australia, it's the Writer's Marketplace, produced by QUP.

Unfortunately, these books can be expensive, especially if you want to submit to areas of the world outside of your own – you will have to pay more for imported books. If you possibly can, find someone else who has already bought them. Or go your local library, which should stock them in the reference section.

It doesn't really matter if they're out of date – you can always confirm contact details later. Contrary to what you might hear, publishers are not too 'prickly' about getting their names wrong – the turnover of staff is so high nowadays it's hard for anyone to keep up! Agents, though, can be a little more sensitive. They expect you to have done a degree of homework before you contact them.

If you are worried that your manuscript won't end up with the right person, make a quick phone call to the publishing house and ask whose name you should address your query. Talking to the reception desk is sufficient. Not all editors take kindly to cold calls from authors. Agents again, are different. Sometimes they prefer a direct pitch over the phone.

Make a list of all the publishers and agents you think will be interested in your work. Target specifically. It really is a waste of time (and postage) to send your manuscripts to inappropriate companies and individuals. Think about what genre your work might fall into and then match it with the genres that the recipients handle. That way, you'll save yourself a lot of time and heartache.

Agent or Publisher?

You will need to decide what's most important to you. Do you want to go it alone? Or do you want someone else to deal with the business side of things?

There's no real problem with sending your manuscript to publishers direct, although many say they prefer you to use an agent.

It's rare nowadays that publishers will publish a first book from an un-agented submission. There are many reasons for this, not least that agents are considered by most publishers to be a necessary foil between the writer and themselves.

This is partly because agents spend their lives sorting through bad books to find the good ones – something the publisher is increasingly unable to find the time for. Also, many individuals in the industry simply prefer dealing with someone not too close to the writing.

Publishers feel they can be more honest, pragmatic and realistic about a book's chances of success when talking to an intermediary. That way they don't risk hurting a writer's feelings. And in business terms, publishers feel more confident that the agent will understand how the money and contracts work.

Submission

To start submitting to agents and publishers you need to think in terms of having a "submission pack".

This will include the following:

1. *Your introductory letter*
2. *Your biography*
3. *A short synopsis of your novel.*
4. *The first three chapters of your novel.*
5. *Return postage*

Intro Letter

This is the first thing your recipient will look at – it's therefore imperative you make this slick, professional looking and in faultless English.

Always use clean white paper in A4 or quarto size. If your printer is not printing cleanly then get it fixed. Don't send anything through the post you would not want to receive. Never use colored paper or weird fonts.

You need say very little. Any more than 100 words is excessive. Just introduce yourself, your book and mention that it is offered for publication. You might mention too why you think your book is especially relevant to the market place but be careful this might be taken the wrong way. It is the recipient's job to make those kinds of judgments and he/she might not take kindly to being lectured to.

As far as your intro letter's content goes, take a look at the following example. Okay, it's short to the point of abruptness but it does get all the necessary information across quickly and efficiently.

E O'Connell
Publishing Co Pty Ltd
PO Box 0000
NY 0000

(Date)

Dear Emily,

Please find enclosed a synopsis and sample chapters of my latest work,

"Title"

It's a 115,000 word supernatural thriller, offered for publication.
I have also enclosed my biography.
If you'd like to see a full copy of the MS, I'd be very happy to send it to you with return postage.
There's an SAE for your reply.
Many thanks for your time.

Yours sincerely,

Peter Chadwick

A letter like this shows that you are professional and don't like to waste anybody's time. After all, Emily probably looks at a hundred of these letters a day. It's pretty obvious to her what your letter was going to say, even before she opened the envelope.

Unless you have something riveting to say, keep it short and sweet. Never try to sell the book or your writing, or explain something you feel the reader should know first. If your manuscript doesn't work on its own terms, without any prior introduction, you shouldn't be sending it out!

Biography

This one page document will list all the main achievements in your life that have a relevancy to your writing. Don't mention trivialities like your jobs or hobbies unless they have a specific bearing on your fiction. For instance, if your lead character is a postman, and you are too, it might be worth mentioning – though it's not imperative.

However, if you're a politician or a celebrity, it's definitely worth mentioning.

Famous names carry great weight in the publishing industry nowadays. Celebrities can sell their shopping lists. The rest of us have it a little harder.

In your biography, mention your successes. List any writing competitions you might have won (however minor) and anything at all you might have had published.

Remember that one page is sufficient. Any more looks like bragging.

The object here is not to blind your reader with your accomplishments. The idea is to make your novel seem like a natural extension of your life – and that you are more than qualified to tell a good story well.

Agents like to know where your manuscripts have been. They don't like surprises when calling someone in the industry about your work. It's best to list previous relationships with publishers and agents even if the relationship didn't work out for the best.

Amateurs tend to list their achievements chronologically like a work CV. In the creative field, this can look bad if you have great gaps where you seem to have achieved nothing in your writing. The more professional you become, the shorter the descriptions of your achievements you need. Hence, even if you're not hugely successful, it makes sense to appear so – by keeping your biog short and punchy. Like this:

Sandra Midden is a popular crime prevention speaker in her hometown of Penney Bush, Arkansas. Her short story, "The Midnight Cuckoo" won the 2009 Wheatsheaf Prize. When not looking after her three young children – and her husband - she writes detective fiction based on her close relationship with the local police department. She is also a keen collector of political memorabilia.

You'll notice that the biography is written in the third person – a common technique I would recommend.

Synopsis

Most writers consider this the hardest thing they'll ever have to do – that is, break down their novel to its key elements and summarize them into less than 2000 words. Even this is considered long. Movie synopses – used to generate millions of dollars – are generally less than 200 words long.

For a reasonably complex novel I would recommend no more than around 750 words.

This is short, I know, but the reality is that your synopsis will probably be read by many more individuals at publishing houses than your manuscript. It's therefore important to make it snappy, well paced and a riveting read.

Many writers are completely stumped when it comes to writing synopses. They don't know what to leave in, what to omit, whether to tell the ending, leave out minor characters and sub plots... the list goes on.

If you've written you book 'the easy way' you should now be able to go back to your original '10-point plan' for your novel. I would recommend you use this as a starting point, rather than doing a synopsis from scratch.

Contrary to what you might think, the purpose of a synopsis is not to tell the story of your novel. If it does that too, all well and good. However, the main purpose of a synopsis is to get people interested in your work. Books are bought and sold on their synopses. The sad fact is, people don't have time to read whole novels nowadays, especially in the publishing industry.

The synopsis will be the 'pitch' that will do the rounds of the publishers' marketing meetings. If it's good and passes the scrutiny of the meeting's attendees, it will then go to the editorial department and on the strength of the synopsis alone, a real live editor might read your first three chapters.

So – how's it done?

You've read the backs of paperbacks? Of course you have. Find one now and take a look. Okay. The truth of it? The blurb there is often written by marketing and copywriting people that have never read the book, although they probably have read the synopsis and been at meetings where the book was discussed.

In order to write the 'pitch', they pick up pertinent elements of the book they think will grab a potential reader's attention, and write a compelling précis.

For your synopsis, that's what you need to do.

Imagine you're making a movie promo.

You want excitement, suspense, intrigue... and you want to get it across in the shortest time possible. Most of all you want a sense of anticipation. You want to make the reader feel the next most important thing their life is to read your book. They cannot go on without it!

You need to set up questions in the reader's mind – quickly – questions they cannot possibly answer without flicking back to page one and reading your book.

When you're telling the story of your novel, remember that you need a sense of urgency. You cannot waste a single word. Remove qualifiers and unnecessary adverbs, write in the present tense to achieve immediacy, and tell the whole story. It's cheating to have a cliff-hanger in a synopsis.

The three main elements you need to get across in your synopsis are theme, characters and plot. The theme can be stated outright. The pursuit of money causes grief. Murder has consequences unforeseen. Duty cannot be resolved with love. Whatever.

Then get your characters in - early. Describe who is in your book, their motivations and the obstacles to their agendas. How do the characters interact? Tell what exciting things happen when they get together and start telling the story — succinctly, with passion and enthusiasm.

Keep going, building the excitement, the sense of jeopardy and urgency until you reach the climax.

When you've finished, re-read your synopsis several times. The golden rule is: if it's boring, chop it out, even if it's just a word or a phrase. If it reads slow, get rid of it!

Your synopsis should be a roller-coaster read: fun, thrilling, and nail-bitingly exciting.

The First Three Chapters

There is no rigid rule about how much you send of your manuscript, except that 99% of the industry doesn't want the whole thing. Don't be disheartened by this. It works in your favor. Mailing manuscripts is expensive. Sending just a section is much cheaper.

Three chapters is the industry standard. It doesn't have to be the first three but if you've written a good book, the most compelling storytelling should be at the beginning of your novel. If you find you are scratching around looking for good bits, you might need to review your entire manuscript!

If your chapters are very long — say 25,000 words or so, then just one or two chapters will be enough. Most editors won't read more than a few pages anyway. After all, how long does it take to realize if you like a book or a writer? About a page and half probably, slightly less if the story seems a little obscure or slow.

Remember that the only person who will read the whole of your actual manuscript is an editor – and this person is usually not the person you send your submission to.

It works like this. A submissions editor, let's call her Jane, screens out about every 99 submissions in every 100. She'll send out all the rejection letters. The 1 in 100 Jane thinks has potential she will send to an editor, say a guy called Derek. He is the real live person who edits and proofreads books for a living.

Note this, because it's important. Unless Derek is overridden by a publishing house director or by the marketing department, it is Derek who will decide whether your novel is worthy of his time and attention, and therefore whether it will be published.

Bear in mind that Derek is probably a frustrated writer who thinks he could have written whatever you have done better. Your work literally needs to shine like a beacon to impress a guy like Derek.

So make sure you have checked and rechecked everything a hundred times on the pages you submit. Spelling, grammar, formatting, sense, nonsense, themes, characters, plotting, foreshadowing – everything should be as perfect as you can get it. Don't worry that the rest of the manuscript isn't up to the same standard – you can worry about that later – when they've offered you a deal! Seriously...

Don't let the idea of 'Derek' intimidate you. Think about it. If he knew what sold and what didn't, he'd be writing best-selling novels himself.

The fact is most best sellers spring out of the blue – nobody can predict them. Really – absolutely nobody! The trick is to play the game and do what every self-respecting author does: cross your fingers and hope like hell your book becomes flavor of the month – this month!

The more books you write, of course, the more chance you have of achieving this end.

The best advice is, after each book, send out your submissions and get back to writing.

Don't leave it too long before the next book – you need to get your juices flowing quickly otherwise you'll start to worry. And, as I often point out, worrying is the worst thing a writer can do.

So don't give yourself the chance. Just write.

Return Postage

It seems absurd in the 21st Century that so many publishers insist on paper submissions and then proceed to send them back to you!

Apparently, there is a copyright issue here. If a writer can prove that a publisher once held an electronic version of his or her book and the publisher subsequently publishes a similar book, the complainant, assuming the writer takes them to court, is likely to win the case.

It's a mistake to get paranoid about it but ideas do get 'recycled' all the time. A publishing person might take on board your idea – only to reject it - and then completely unwittingly be open to the very same idea from someone else.

Unless a publisher is blatantly plagiarizing an author's work, there's very little a new writer can do about this. Even copyrighting your material won't help you - before you're famous.

On the positive side, your material is theoretically copyrighted from the moment it leaves your head. Try not to worry about plagiarism. Certainly don't let it stop you writing and submitting. It's pointless to lose sleep over having your ideas poached. It happens very rarely – or sometimes just appears that way.

Besides, it's not all about ideas anyway. Good writing is about how you deal with those ideas. That's what makes you different, sellable and unique.

Multiple Submissions

The industry advice on this varies. Certain individuals, like agents, want to feel they're being targeted by an earnest writer who has no other interest in anyone else.

Unfortunately, this can add months to your search for an agent.

There's nothing inherently wrong with a scattergun approach with publishers though.

After all, the likelihood of one in fifty wanting your book makes it seem absurd to submit to them one at a time.

If you do receive an offer from one publisher, don't immediately call all the others and tell them to ignore your submission. Don't believe anything until the money's in the bank and you've signed the dotted line.

The Waiting Game

Nowadays, most replies will be back with you within 6 to 12 weeks.

Logic implies most if not all will be rejections. That's okay. There are a hundred reasons why your submission was rejected and only one of them will be because of the quality of your writing.

Mostly it will be to do with the mood of the editor, office politics, the price of cotton, the whims and vagaries of the publishing house's aspirations, and what they're planning to sell in the next couple of years or whatever.

Most publishing houses have a large list of authors already on their books. They'll be promoting them first. They will very rarely take on a new author. Perhaps one or two a year. That's what you're up against. Don't take rejection personally.

Advances

As times goes by, cash advances for first time authors are getting smaller.

Indeed, some publishers (even bona fide ones) want money from you. They might offer you a few thousand and then tell you that editing your manuscript will cost you $2000, which you must agree to forfeit from your advance! Unfortunately, this is becoming an increasingly common practice in the US.

Study carefully at any deal you're offered. Get a lawyer or an agent to look it over for you.

Next Steps

Should you follow up on your submission? The general advice given on this is that it's usually okay to phone after 6 to 8 weeks and chase a response. This is not altogether true. If an agent or publisher wants you, they will call you.

So, should you call? I'd say no. It's considered unprofessional. Only novices and desperate hacks do it. And working writers leave their agents to call.

Publishers and agents are generally overworked and underpaid and really don't have the time to talk to novices. They're usually too busy working on projects that need to be finished yesterday.

Their other duties like looking at new talent, discussing it with others and making proposals at meetings take second place to their core business – that is: selling the books they already own. Don't annoy them by constantly asking for advice or feedback.

Nothing is more guaranteed to get you blacklisted!

The Truth of It

There are as many ways to get published as there are authors. There is no 'one sure-fire way' that will work every time. However, one thing is clear. It's all about persistence. The longer you beat a path to the door of the publishing industry, the more you get your name around and, eventually, the more seriously you are taken.

Of course getting published is about the quality of your work but it's also about your commitment. The industry wants to know you're in for the long haul – and not just the quick buck.

Self Promotion

Okay, let's imagine your book has been accepted for publication. Then comes the process of negotiation, editing, rewriting and finally scheduling for release. This process can take anything up to two years. Two years?!? I hear you cry. Yep. That's the norm.

You'd better start writing your follow up books now. Don't sit out the time and wait for fame and glory. Your publisher and agent will want you to have more material – and they will want to be reassured that you are a career writer.

What can you do when the book finally appears? Your publisher might have already thought of some of the following ideas but it does no harm at all for you to consider and act independently or in conjunction with them. Don't expect them to have done anything!

Their initial enthusiasm for your book may have cooled and you might find your novel assigned to someone who will only give it about a week's worth of publicity and then move on.

Freebies

You will want to send out a good many free copies to various people in the industry and the media to build momentum, get feedback and hopefully receive some reviews you can use to push the book.

If you send your book to other authors, don't ask them to review it, or even read it. The best approach is to offer it to them as a gift. Let them choose to reply to you – better still let them reply to your agent.

Some authors will agree to write a favorable review for a fee. The ethics of this are questionable at best but it will be up to you decide whether you go for it. It's probably best not to encourage this kind of thing.

Don't forget to send your book to people you already know. In some ways this is harder than sending to people you don't know. It's like laying open your soul. But we often forget that the people closest to us are those that can help us the most.

Also send copies to people in professions related to your novel. For instance, if your book is a crime novel, why not send a free copy to the local police department? You might receive valuable feedback or even a rave review!

Send free copies to newspaper and magazine reviewers, on and off the Net, in fact anyone who might be able to say something nice. Don't forget to ask permission to use testimonials. Some professionals can be quite tetchy about bandying their names around to promote your book – even after they've said something positive. Get their written permission first is the golden rule.

Send copies to radio stations with perhaps a note saying you'd be willing to come in and talk about a certain topic. If you can, get the names of the producers, not the presenters, as it is the program producers that decide a show's content.

Get a fax machine. This is useful for sending out press releases. Always try to make press releases news worthy and relevant. It's next to pointless sending out a one-page sheet with the title of your book on it, announcing its presence. Try to think of something a newspaper would be interested in - how your book's theme is relevant to a piece of news perhaps. Don't worry if you are universally ignored at first. It's the way of the modern world. Apparently editors will often ignore the first three press releases from someone before they latch on to a story.

Think local – organize bookshop signings, perhaps tours of the shops in your state or town. Could you turn your book into a workshop? Could you talk about the craft of writing for an hour or two to other authors? Could you give a presentation at your local writers' center? Phone them and ask what they expect from speakers. Drop books off for them to sell or give away to other writers, writers' groups or the passing public. You never know where your free copies might end up.

Quite often you can be years into your career when somebody famous will say "Ah yes, I remember your first book. I found it in such and such a place and read it." Or even, "I've been watching your progress for years. I knew you'd make it one day." You are never as alone as you might think.

Social Networking

I've deliberately left social networking online out of the picture until now because, despite all the hype to the contrary, the jury is still out on whether active social networking actually does sell more than half a dozen books.

Certainly there is a case to be made for an online presence - when you already have a following. But having done an immense amount of research on this issue, I'm yet to be convinced that spamming Facebook, Twitter, Google+ and all the other social networking sites actually creates an appreciable spike in sales.

Sometimes it can help. Mostly it's a waste of precious writing time.

To me, writers' time is better spent writing than using hours and days building 'social proof' - whatever that means.

My advice is that if you enjoy social networking, by all means do it. Just don't expect it to generate bestsellers for you!

Self Publicity

Authors are finding that getting a deal and sitting back to collect royalties isn't working any more. Authors have to work at getting their name and their work noticed. And it's hard nowadays.

Now, if you've got a publishing deal, you're going to do all this work for a book that sells for maybe $20, of which you get say, two dollars, if you're lucky. Your agent will also get a dollar fifty and the rest goes to the publisher. Doesn't seem fair does it? Well, it does if you sell fifty thousand and above. But how likely is that?

When you sign to a publisher, your advance can be anything from nothing to about ten thousand dollars. Let's assume you're somewhere in the middle.

Say you get $5,000 for your first book. That means you will have to sell at least 10,000 books to cover your advance – before you earn any royalties. The publisher is banking on this, otherwise he would not have offered you this money.

First runs of books are notoriously small. Publishers like to test the water first. They may print just a thousand, half of which they will give away as promotional aids. Then if the book is well received and gets a couple of nice reviews they will print some more, say 2,000 or perhaps 10,000.

Now, if the book sits on shelves gathering dust (i.e. they don't get any more orders from the book chain-stores), they won't print any more. Three months down the line and the books start coming back to the printers. The publisher has two options. One, tear them all up into pulp and make some more books or, sell them as remainders at a fraction of the cost.

By the way, you will probably not see any of the profit from remaindered books because the publisher reserves the right not to give you any in this (all too common) scenario.

Now try selling your second book to the same publisher. Either they will say "Hey but you never even made us our money back on your first book," or, more than likely, "Go to hell!"

Okay, this sounds bleak. You're different. Your book is destined for the big time – or at least a cult following.

You might be lucky. Your publisher and agent might agree with you and will keep releasing your books in the belief your following will grow. It happens – especially with fantasy and SF authors. But mostly the industry can't support this kind of activity – they already have back catalogues of hungry authors that are all hanging on, one book at a time, vying for position and notoriety, and a little bit of fame.

You now have three options.

1. Find a supportive partner or sugar daddy that will support you with no immediate financial gain in sight.

2. Keep at the day job until you have a best-seller.

3. Self publish

Yeah, I know self-publishing this has an awful stigma to it but just for a moment think about it.

If you're going to have to do all that self-promotion anyway, wouldn't it be better if you could earn 70% to 90% of each sale?

The best thing? Once you've sold your book to all the people you wanted to – it's still yours to sell to a publisher!

Don't get me wrong. I'm not talking about Vanity Publishing – that's a whole different ballgame.

That's where you pay a vanity press to have anywhere from 1,000 to 10,000 of your book printed – at exorbitant prices – and usually badly done. No editorial support, no advice on covers, artwork etc. Nothing.

The favorite scam of these people is to contact you after 3-6 months and ask you to now start paying for storage. Of course, you won't want to so they'll let you have them at a discount price – say 50% of the cover price. You do the sums and realize you'll be working like a dog to sell all these books for the rest of your life so, you say no... they then tell you they will have to charge you for destroying them, at say 25% of the cost.

Whatever you do - don't get caught up in it!

No, by self-publishing, I mean finding a printer who will work with you to produce a book cheaply as a one off run. Either that or get a great cover design and self publish with Amazon and Createspace - a great free option these days for any new writer!

If the book does well, publishers and agents will be beating a path to you!

Final Word

If you want to succeed, take action, think laterally and always be on the lookout for a new way to promote yourself and your book.

Good luck, keep writing, and never give up. You're always closer to success than you think!

You can get lots of my free writing resources and my weekly newsletter by subscribing to my website: www.easywaytowrite.com

Rob Parnell

After-Word

Now I need to ask a favor.

If you have any luck with the advice in this book, I want to know about it! I'd be grateful for any feedback that I might be able to use for the next edition of this book.

Please – feel free to email me: rob@easywaytowrite.com

You may also like to join my Kindle Review Club.
You get free Kindle books from me to beta read, review and keep.
http://easywaytowrite.com/Kindle_Review.Club.html

FURTHER READING

Below are listed some excellent books that will inspire and motivate you. I've included a few self-help books that will help you achieve any of your dreams.

Becoming a Writer - Dorothea Brande

On Writing - Stephen King

How to Write a Damn Good Novel - James N Frey

Hypnotic Writing - Joe Vitale

The Elements of Style - Strunk and White

Unlimited Power - Anthony Robbins

Feel the Fear and Do It Anyway - Susan Jeffers

Creative Visualization - Shakti Gawain

You Can't Afford the Luxury of a Negative Thought - John Roger & Peter McWilliams

Rob Parnell's Nonfiction

The Easy Way to Write a Novel That Sells

The Easy Way to Write Short Stories That Sell

The Easy Way to Write Crime Fiction That Sells

The Easy Way to Write Fantasy That Sells

The Easy Way to Write Romance That Sells

The Easy Way to Write Thrillers That Sell

The Easy Way to Write Horror That Sells

The Easy Way to Write An Autobiography That Sells

The Easy Way to Write Hollywood Screenplays That Sell

The Easy Way to Write TV Shows That Sell

The Writer and The Hero's Journey

Easy Cash Writing: How to Make a Living as a Freelance Writer

From Zero to Hero: How To Make Living Writing Fiction

The Art of Story

Elements of Story

Fast and Furious #1: Writing for Amazon and Kindle
Fast and Furious #2: Writing for Amazon and Kindle

Fast and Furious #3: Mastering Amazon and Kindle

The Easy Way to Get Rich: 21 Keys to Lasting Prosperity

The Easy Way to Lose Weight and Stay Thin Forever

Make Your Writing Sparkle (with Robyn Opie Parnell)

Fiction by Rob Parnell

Purge

Kindred

Willow

Nine Tales

Sherlock Holmes: Zombie Slayer #1 - The Revenant Problem

Sherlock Holmes: Zombie Slayer #2 - The Ugly Experiment

Sherlock Holmes: Zombie Slayer #2 - Boys Will Be Boys

Connect With Rob Parnell

Easy Way To Write Blog
http://easywaytowrite.blogspot.com.au/

Rob's Author Page
http://www.amazon.com/Rob-Parnell/e/B006QPU4NQ/

Rob's Twitter
http://twitter.com/robparnell

Rob's Facebook
http://www.facebook.com/rob.parnell
http://www.facebook.com/rob.parnell.106

Rob's Goodreads
http://goodreads.com/robparnell

Rob's Youtube Channel
http://www.youtube.com/robparnell2008

Rob's imdb
http://www.imdb.com/name/nm1239587/

Rob's iTunes:
http://itunes.apple.com/us/artist/rob-parnell/

ABOUT THE AUTHOR

Rob Parnell has been writing since he was five years old. He writes every day without fail - it's like a compulsion - and he still hasn't run out of things to say...

His preferred genre is the thriller - sometimes with a supernatural edge - in which he writes short stories, graphic novels, screenplays, and adult thrillers.

In between fiction projects, Rob has written over forty nonfiction self-help titles and has been published all over the world for the last fifteen years. Also a musician and composer, singer, media producer, and budding movie maker, Rob is ecstatically happy to be married to Robyn Opie Parnell, his savior and his best friend.